A GIFT OF MANY COLORS

KEREN KESHET
THE RAINBOW FOUNDATION
1999–2019

TONY PROSCIO

WICKED SON

2023

A WICKED SON BOOK
An Imprint of Post Hill Press
ISBN: 979-8-88845-037-6
ISBN (eBook): 979-8-88845-038-3

A Gift of Many Colors:
The First Two Decades of Keren Keshet—The Rainbow Foundation
© 2023 by Tony Proscio
All Rights Reserved

Cover and interior design by Richard Ljoenes Design LLC

Post Hill Press
New York • Nashville
posthillpress.com

Published in the United States of America
10 9 8 7 6 5 4 3 2 1

CONTENTS

CHAPTER I

'A GREAT ARCH IN THE SKY'

On a mild August afternoon in his 53rd year, Sanford Charles Bernstein, creator of the investment-management colossus that still bears his name, stepped for the first time into Lincoln Square Synagogue, on Manhattan's west side, to say Kaddish for his father. The younger Mr. Bernstein was, at that moment, at the threshold of a Jewish awakening, inspired by his father's devotion, that would soon transform his life. Within days of that first visit, the synagogue's celebrated rabbi, Shlomo Riskin, began guiding him on a course of Jewish learning, lasting many years, that led him to adopt the Hebrew name Zalman Chaim and become a fixture of Lincoln Square's spiritual and social life. Some 15 years later, he and his wife, Mem, would make Aliyah and anchor their lives securely in the Land of Israel.

By the time he retired from his firm in 1993, Mr. Bernstein had taken on a new career that he pursued every bit as passionately as he had that of finance. He embarked on a mission of philanthropy aimed at strengthening the Jewish people by cultivating a more widespread

understanding and observance of Jewish customs, deeper appreciation of Jewish culture, and stronger bonds among all Jews, regardless
of their backgrounds or degrees of religious faith. He founded two
ambitious Jewish charities: the AVI CHAI Foundation, a grantmaking
institution dedicated to promoting Jewish learning and solidarity, and
the Tikvah Fund, a think-tank and leadership-development organization that also funds Shalem College, a liberal arts institution based
in Jerusalem.

Unlike his company, neither charity bore his name (AVI CHAI is
Hebrew for "My Father Lives," and Tikvah for "Hope"), and he routinely declined to be honored or spotlighted for his philanthropy. Yet
both organizations were intensely personal undertakings and con-
sumed most of his creative energies in his last two decades of life.
As chairman of AVI CHAI, in particular, Mr. Bernstein immersed
himself in the details of designing and funding projects, personally
overseeing not just the selection of grantees and the awarding of
grants but the creation and staffing of new organizations, the conduct
of research, the analysis of problems and assessment of solutions, and
(to the frequent exhaustion of foundation employees) even the keeping of records and documentation of meetings, conversations, and
decisions.

At first, a prime reason for Mr. Bernstein's obsessive involvement
in every aspect of his philanthropy was a belief that people who work
in foundations sometimes end up reinterpreting the donor's intentions
through the prism of their own predilections. He therefore maintained only a small staff at the AVI CHAI Foundation and relied mostly
on a hand-picked board of trustees for advice on where and how to
allocate money. At the core of this governing body were three people
designated as members of the foundation, who held near-total control
over the actions of the larger board. The three were Mr. Bernstein

himself and two peers in the top ranks of corporate leadership and philanthropy: Arthur W. Fried and Samuel J. Silberman, commonly known as Buddy. Mr. Fried was then director-general of Yad Hanadiv, the Rothschild Foundation in Israel, but before that he had been managing director and chief financial officer of Lehman Brothers. Buddy Silberman had been CEO of his family's tobacco business, Consolidated Cigar, until it was sold in 1968. Thereafter, he devoted much of his considerable wealth to philanthropy, a good portion of it for Jewish causes.

In later years, and especially as cancer eroded his health and sapped his energy, Mr. Bernstein deferred more and more to his two fellow members to lead his charities and keep them focused on their founding mission. In 1998, as his condition worsened, he passed the AVI CHAI chairmanship to Mr. Fried. His earlier fears of mission drift had not disappeared—at one point, he told Mr. Fried that he hoped AVI CHAI would expend all its assets within the lifetime of its current board, so that it would not pass into the hands of unknown successors. (At the end of 2019, it honored that wish and ceased its grantmaking.) Still, he had come to bestow on his fellow members such complete confidence that in his periods of gravest illness he was able to step away from the organization without reservations.

Zalman Bernstein died of lymphoma on January 6, 1999, at the age of 72. By that time, he had named Mr. Fried and Mr. Silberman as his executors, along with his wife, Mem Dryan Bernstein. She would also succeed her husband as the third member of AVI CHAI and join the board of the Tikvah Fund. To these three executors Mr. Bernstein delegated an astonishing breadth of discretion over the use of his charitable wealth, with only the most minimal instructions for allocating half of the money and almost no direction on how to use the rest. In a Letter of Allocation less than three months before his death, Mr. Bernstein asked his friends and his wife to give at least 40 percent of the estate's charitable assets to AVI CHAI and at least 10 percent to Tikvah. Beyond that, he wrote, "The balance of the assets distributable for charitable purposes shall be distributed to other charitable organizations which you select."

Asked why her husband—a man who had spent decades minutely overseeing his charities to keep them scrupulously faithful to his wishes—would abdicate all control at the end of his life, Mem Bernstein could offer only the simplest answer: "He trusted us. I don't know what else to say. He trusted us, that's all."

The estate's liquid assets accumulated slowly, with just over $32 million becoming available in 1999. The executors set aside nearly one-third of that amount to fund the acquisition and renovation of offices at 1015 Park Avenue in Manhattan, most of which would be made available rent-free to AVI CHAI. Another $12.5 million followed in early 2000, but soon thereafter, Sanford C. Bernstein & Co. was sold to Alliance Capital Management for a reported $3.5 billion. From that point, the money available for charity multiplied quickly. To distribute the portion that would not be passed through to AVI CHAI and Tikvah, Mr. Fried, Mr. Silberman, and Mrs. Bernstein chose to create a foundation and infuse it with a mission that both honored Zalman Bernstein's charitable spirit and embodied the ideals, wisdom, and expertise that the three executors brought to their task. Although there was no legal need for a new foundation—charitable distributions could have been made directly from the estate—the trustees concluded that a foundation would give them the structure and latitude to carry on a deliberate, measured form of giving, with no pressure to allocate resources quickly, and with a formal emphasis on a few designated areas of philanthropy.

On July 8, a certificate of incorporation was filed with the State of New York for a new grantmaking institution called Keren Keshet, Hebrew for "the Rainbow Foundation." The new organization's lyrical mission statement borrowed partly from an earlier one that Mr. Silberman had originally written to govern AVI CHAI. But in this version, Mr. Fried drafted additional paragraphs to clarify both the new foundation's name and the values that would guide it:

The word *keshet*, or rainbow, has been included in the name of the Corporation because it serves as the biblical sign of the protecting covenant between G-d and every living soul. The distinguished Rabbinic personality of the 19th century Samson Rafael Hirsch speaks eloquently of the phenomenon of a great arch in the sky which follows the rain. . . .

When examining the physical properties of a rainbow, one finds a single white light shining through a moisture-laden sky. The pure light is refracted by the moisture and spreads into seven degrees of colors, from the richest red at the top to the darkest violet at the bottom. But the lines or hues between the seven colors are blurred, one mixing into the next. Could the *keshet* possibly be meant to reflect the wide variety and rich hues of the Jewish People, each person selecting his or her own particular shade of Judaism, but nevertheless forming part of one People, the original bright white light?

The rainbow unites each of the colors and blurs their connection and, in so doing, creates one common bond of purity and

peace, all fragments of a shared heritage and tradition, all refracted rays of a culture which has stood the test of now three
millennia. . . .

The purposes for which the Corporation is formed and the nature
of the activities to be conducted shall serve to enhance the common
bonds, while respecting the distinctions, among all peoples of the
Jewish faith, and ensure that Jewish culture, in all its many manifestations, is preserved and strengthened through study, increased
awareness and understanding, and practice.

The text then went on to reassert the core purposes embedded in
AVI CHAI's mission: to encourage Jews to embrace Jewish "observance
and lifestyle," to promote mutual understanding and a common identity among "Jews of different religious backgrounds and commitments to observance," and to advance the well-being of the State of
Israel. In both letter and spirit, the statement painted an entire rainbow of philanthropic colors onto a very large canvas, encompassing
nearly everything that enriches and preserves Jewish life.

Some foundations' mission statements are written with the intent
of narrowing and disciplining their work. For example, the Robert
Wood Johnson Foundation restricts its grantmaking to the fields of
health and healthcare, and the Kellogg Foundation aims all its work
at the well-being of children and their families. Other statements, by
contrast, seem intentionally designed to impose no limits at all, apart
from those that govern tax exemption. The Rockefeller Foundation,
for instance, was launched with a mission to "promote the well-being
of humanity throughout the world" and has kept that mission for
more than a century—during which the foundation's actual activities
have shifted profoundly from one decade to the next. The John D. and
Catherine T. MacArthur Foundation is committed to "building a

more just, verdant, and peaceful world," which arguably rules out grants to develop new weapons systems or herbicides, but plainly tolerates nearly everything else.

Keren Keshet's statement of purposes deliberately avoided both of these extremes. On one hand, it adhered to a resolute focus on promoting Jewish culture, observance, and identity. It was unambiguous about excluding anything that might alienate Jews from one another or distance them from their cultural heritage or from the Jewish state. On the other hand, its invocation of "Jewish culture, in all its many manifestations," and of "study, awareness, understanding, and practice" left open whole encyclopedias of religious, cultural, and social undertakings. Even while maintaining a strict obedience to its mission, Keren Keshet could—and in fact did—support small charities and big enterprises; artistic programs both popular and refined; solemn research and lighthearted public festivity; purely secular study and rigorous religious training; the creation of both libraries and playing fields; and a panoply of other projects in technology, medicine, journalism, and literature, all in service to some facet of "Jewish culture in all its many manifestations."

This effort to define a mission that was clear but not overly restrictive was partly an outgrowth of the way Mrs. Bernstein and Mr. Fried intended to operate (Mr. Silberman, already in failing health when the foundation was incorporated, died in 2000, at age 84). The two trustees wanted neither a big staff nor a roster of strategic protocols tying fixed budgets to pre-ordained lines of grantmaking. They wanted maximum flexibility, untethered either to the "strategic" or "responsive" models of philanthropy.

In the former approach, a foundation sets out to attack the root causes of some social problem that it has defined, usually based on extensive research. After mapping out a strategy, often thick with "logic models" and "Theories of Change," a strategic foundation may spend a decade or more trying to pull multiple levers of causation in the hope of eventually solving its chosen problem. By contrast, with a "responsive" approach to philanthropy, a foundation doesn't decide how a problem should be solved but instead makes itself available to meet the needs of frontline charities that it considers the most important or effective. It supports those grantees in whatever way makes them stronger, within the foundation's means. Nonetheless, identifying the "most important" and "most effective," and negotiating the best form and scale of support for each, usually call for a lot of time and expertise.

Either approach (and many foundations combine the two) can require a sizable staff to do the research, design programs, reconnoiter the field, negotiate deliverables, conduct evaluations, issue reports, and otherwise ensure that the foundation is making the right grants for the right reasons. Mr. Fried and Mrs. Bernstein considered both of these versions of philanthropy too expensive, labor-intensive, and confining.

"First and foremost, this was a labor of love," Mrs. Bernstein observed some years later. "It was our chance to express our philanthropic desires without having to answer to anybody else. We meant it to give us the ability to do whatever we wanted to." Unlike the highly structured programs of AVI CHAI and Tikvah, with their diverse boards and explicit program objectives, Keren Keshet would be an outgrowth solely of its two trustees' judgments about need and opportunity in whatever branch of Jewish communal life caught their attention. "And that's exactly what we did," she continued. "It was fun. It was creative. It was energizing."

Keeping the staff small was an important part of keeping the foundation flexible and satisfying. Both trustees played many other roles in philanthropy—including as highly active board members of AVI CHAI and Tikvah, but also in other leadership roles in Jewish communal life. They relished the opportunity to support Judaism and Jewish causes that didn't fit neatly into the well-defined missions of the other two Bernstein charities, but they were not prepared to devote themselves to managing a bureaucracy.

On the contrary, among their first decisions, even before Keren Keshet was incorporated, was to recruit a principal staff person who would see that the foundation's business was transacted in an orderly, simple, and straightforward way. They wanted a smart generalist who would ensure that decisions were implemented faithfully and that organizational responsibilities were discharged fully and prudently— but not someone who would feel called on to improvise, create unnecessary work, or impose needless burdens on grantees.

In the early months of administering Mr. Bernstein's estate, they had been relying on one of his longtime assistants for this kind of help, but she preferred to stay on at the investment company rather than making the leap into philanthropy. As an alternative, she recommended a lifelong friend, Linda B. Sakacs, who was then chief of staff at a technology recruiting firm but was looking to make a change. Before that, Mrs. Sakacs had been an aide to the president of Citibank for well over a decade and was at ease with the demands of administering large amounts of money and multiple organizational relationships. Mr. Fried and Mrs. Bernstein liked her immediately and soon made an offer. But she had just one reservation, and she wondered if they might be concerned about it too: She isn't Jewish.

It didn't faze them. Although an Irish Catholic director of a Jewish foundation might seem superficially odd, expertise in Judaism wasn't really a requirement of the job. The two trustees intended to make their own decisions about Jewish causes to support and could, at any time, call on battalions of other communal leaders with expertise in practically any aspect of Jewish life. What they needed was someone who could run a tight ship, keep many lines of work humming productively, and deal diplomatically with a wide range of grantee personalities and needs. Mrs. Sakacs not only met all those requirements but was uncommonly eager to learn the technicalities of philanthropy, with its various legal and regulatory obligations, potential stumbling blocks, and peculiar folkways.

As it happened, however, philanthropy wasn't the only new field Mrs. Sakacs would have to learn to navigate. When she started work in April 1999, the trustees were operating temporarily out of Mr. Bernstein's former office in his company's Manhattan headquarters at Fifth Avenue and 59th Street. They were preparing to buy a building of their own, to house both Keren Keshet and AVI CHAI. A closing on the building, at 1015 Park Avenue, took place a few months after her arrival, and thereafter she would be responsible for overseeing the renovations and eventual move-in.

"I felt completely unprepared for that role," she said in a reminiscence many years later. "I'd had no exposure to construction projects, other than a home renovation 20 years prior, and this was, to me, a major project. It was a big challenge, and I didn't have the least idea how to handle it." The building had been designated a historic landmark, a status guaranteed to complicate any renovation project. Beyond that, it had fallen into disrepair after years of deferred maintenance. It would need a small army of specialized contractors to rehabilitate and update nearly every aspect of the building without breaching New York City's famously strict historic preservation rules. Mr. Fried had had extensive experience overseeing big real estate developments—including the construction of Israel's Supreme Court building, which he had funded when he led Yad Hanadiv—and he felt confident that he and the project's construction manager could furnish whatever technical guidance Mrs. Sakacs might need. The months of construction became, she said, "one of the most challenging things I've faced in this job, and it was one of the first things." Nonetheless, the project was completed on time and within budget, and the foundation moved in roughly a year and a half later.

In Israel, Mr. Bernstein's personal assistant had already been extensively involved in his philanthropy and so was happy to stay on as Keren Keshet's Jerusalem staff member. Evan David Feinsilver had begun working for Mr. Bernstein after responding to a newspaper ad in 1996, knowing almost nothing, at that point, about his prospective employer. Although he showed up late for his interview—normally a capital crime in the Bernstein world—he nonetheless won the job and quickly became enamored with it, and with Mr. Bernstein's distinctive approach to philanthropy.

Although many people who had worked for Mr. Bernstein found him forbiddingly critical and demanding, Mr. Feinsilver thought the benefits of enduring the occasional outburst far outweighed the cost. "I had never encountered this kind of thinking, approach, professionalism, business sense, people-sense, the list was long," he wrote later, in a reflection on his first years on the job. "I was eager to learn, and Zalman was eager to teach, and we made a good match." Although he took Mr. Bernstein's death especially hard, the opportunity to continue the Bernstein legacy in Israel appealed to Mr. Feinsilver, who remains at the foundation as this is written, 25 years after the ad first appeared in the newspaper.

Apart from part-time clerical and bookkeeping aides, Linda Sakacs and Evan Feinsilver constituted the entire program staff in Keren Keshet's first four years. Thereafter, the only major addition was that of a full-time CFO in 2003, Yehuda Novick, who would soon come to play a key role in several large projects. Otherwise, the foundation's grantmaking was essentially the work of four people: the two trustees and one person in each of their two offices.

One reason the staff could remain so lean was that the trustees functioned as their own program officers, carrying on a nearly constant reconnaissance for grantmaking opportunities. They traveled widely in the United States and Israel, and later in the former Soviet Union. They drew from their own life experiences and those of their families, and kept a continual lookout for bold ideas championed by people they regarded as "winners"—entrepreneurial leaders with the foresight and drive to produce good results. Without attempting an exhaustive survey of every outstanding Jewish project and program— and without welcoming unsolicited proposals, which would have demanded endless hours for review, assessment, and response—they nonetheless kept antennae out for any promising, inspiring work that might cross their path.

They felt no obligation to guarantee that every dollar or shekel would be put to what some philanthropists call the "highest and best" use—the charitable version of maximizing the return on investment. As Mrs. Bernstein and Mr. Fried saw it, funding a worthwhile activity, producing a valuable result, filling a gaping need for some community or field are all inherently good deeds. To calculate whether the same money, differently used, might fund a somewhat better activity or a more valuable result somewhere else might be intellectually satisfying, but also enormously demanding in both time and resources. In their view, the needs of the Jewish people are plentiful, urgent, and diverse. It is better to meet those needs where and when you happen to find them—and then to give, as Mr. Fried put it, "with warm hands"—than to tarry and temporize while coldly seeking some (probably elusive) perfect use of funds.

Having bestowed on the foundation an eloquent, lofty statement of mission, Mr. Fried nonetheless acknowledged that the trustees' actual principles of giving were, in practice, fairly simple and modest. Asked to name the essential, unwavering rules of grantmaking at Keren Keshet, Mr. Fried listed just three.

"Do good. Don't do bad. And Jewish."

CHAPTER II

BIG DREAMS

Envisioning the Jewish Community
High School of the Bay

Although Mr. Bernstein had set almost no limits on how half his charitable wealth could be used, his executors took care to honor the spirit—Mr. Fried liked the Hebrew word *ruach*—of the donor's lifetime of giving. A few causes that had been dear to Mr. Bernstein also appealed to his widow and Mr. Fried as wellsprings of contemporary Judaism. At the core of these were a handful of Modern Orthodox institutions and spiritual leaders who had helped to energize a new generation of knowledgeable and engaged Jews, including Mr. Bernstein's original Jewish mentor, Shlomo Riskin. Over the years, Keren Keshet would donate nearly $4 million to Ohr Torah Stone, a network of more than two dozen educational and religious organizations founded by Rabbi Riskin. It is devoted to advancing an inviting, welcoming, contemporary understanding of Orthodox Judaism, especially for Jews who, like the young Mr. Bernstein, had become alienated from their heritage.

Similarly, streams of grants supported work by other distinguished

Modern Orthodox rabbis who impressed the Keshet trustees, including Rabbi Riskin's colleague at Lincoln Square Synagogue, Saul Berman. Rabbi Berman's Modern Orthodox education and outreach program Edah received more than $600,000 from Keren Keshet between 2000 and 2009. Rabbi Avi Weiss received a total of $2.5 million over the years for three influential institutions he founded in New York City: the Hebrew Institute of Riverdale, Meorot, and Yeshivat Chovevei Torah.

Rabbi Chaim Brovender, founder of two distinguished yeshivas in Jerusalem, received some $1.5 million to renovate one of them, Midreshet Lindenbaum, an institution of advanced study in Bible and Talmud for women. (Three senior officers of AVI CHAI had studied there, and one classroom at Midreshet Lindenbaum is dedicated to each of them, at Keren Keshet's request). Rabbi Brovender also established the Academy for Torah Initiatives and Direction (ATID), a think tank promoting educational leadership in Modern Orthodoxy. Mrs. Bernstein and Mr. Fried provided $500,000 for ATID between 1999 and 2010. Beit Morasha, a program of advance study for rabbis and educators that had been founded at Mr. Bernstein's behest and originally funded by AVI CHAI, also received $1.3 million from Keren Keshet.

These and at least a dozen other programs became foundation grantees not primarily because Mr. Bernstein had valued and supported them, but more because the trustees of his charitable wealth saw value in the spirit and enterprise with which they were run.

"Take Rabbi Brovender," Mr. Fried said in an interview after more than two decades of grantmaking. "A great teacher. A great man. He was the first to open up gap-year study programs for Orthodox women and men. But our support wasn't about the programs. It was Brovender. You find a jewel, you polish it, you put it in a good setting, you make sure that it continues to sparkle brightly and enliven Jewish lives. But the key is, it's got to be a jewel first."

"We never asked ourselves, 'What would Zalman do?'" Mrs. Bernstein added in the same conversation. "Never. There were a few commitments that Zalman made before he died, and of course we honored those. But other than that, we never supported anything just because he would have. There were outstanding people or programs we were proud to support that happened to have some connection to Zalman. But many others—most of them, really—did not."

––––––––

In fact, the foundation was barely eight months old when it embarked on what would become one of its largest and longest philanthropic projects, involving an institution entirely unconnected to Mr. Bernstein or his philanthropic projects. In early 2000, a new Jewish day school was being planned, with temporary startup space rented from a synagogue in Tiburon, California, north of San Francisco. The planned Jewish Community High School of the Bay expected to start with a single freshman class of about 20 students, and its budget was a shoestring. It had come to the foundation's attention through Mrs. Bernstein's eldest daughter from an earlier marriage, Suzanne Dryan Felson, who was on the board of San Francisco's Jewish Community Federation and a member of a committee searching for a permanent home for the school. The committee, led by the school's founders, Nancy Pechner and Noah Alper, was initially interested in a site in the Sausalito Highlands. At Ms. Felson's urging, they contacted Keren Keshet for help. The foundation offered $50,000 to explore the Sausalito site and see what could be accomplished there, but the property proved unsuitable so quickly that most of the money was never spent. Even so, a big idea was born.

Mrs. Bernstein knew something about creating day schools. She had done it herself, with her then-husband, Hal Dryan, and the philanthropist Jim Joseph, in 1972. Together they established the South Peninsula Hebrew Day School, an outstanding Modern Orthodox elementary and middle school midway between Palo Alto and San Jose. She also knew the Bay Area and its Jewish community—America's fourth largest—from having lived, worked, and raised children there. Although the area boasted several fine Jewish lower schools, the scarcity of high school opportunities was, in her view, a chronic educational and cultural deficit that cried out to be remedied. Research by AVI CHAI had demonstrated that the strongest factor in fortifying a young person's Jewish identity later in life was having completed at least nine years of Jewish education. High school made the bond even stronger. And yet, for most Jewish families in the San Francisco area, that was barely an option.

The Bay Area did have one high school that exceled in both Jewish and general studies, the Lisa Kampner Hebrew Academy. But it was small and, unlike many of the Jewish lower schools, it was a traditional Orthodox institution where non-Orthodox families did not always feel at ease. In any event, with an enrollment in just the dozens each year, the Hebrew Academy was hardly sufficient by itself to serve a region with one-third of a million Jewish residents.[1]

So the idea of a community high school, serving a diverse mix of Jewish families from strictly observant to mostly secular, immediately appealed to both Mrs. Bernstein and Mr. Fried. When the site in Sausalito Highlands fell through, rather than merely canceling the grant, they spent time thinking about what else they could do to help the project move forward. They made another modest grant, to search for a headmaster and pay that person's salary for a year or so. And they were prepared to make a much more substantial contribution to the school if it found its footing and got securely off the ground. But what if it didn't?

One springtime afternoon, during a walk through Central Park, Mr. Fried suggested to Mrs. Bernstein that the matter was too important just to leave to chance. The decision came in a flash.

"I remember it like it was yesterday," he said 20 years later. "We were sitting on a bench in Central Park, saying, 'What can we do? They need so much.' And that's when I said, 'Let's just *do* it. This is an opportunity to put a Jewish community high school in the Bay Area.'" His determination sprang in large part from Mrs. Bernstein's personal connection to the city and its Jewish community and her knowledge of the educational landscape there. "It's a critical need in a community you know," he told her. "You know the place; you know the people; you have children there. Let's *do* it. And we did."

"Arthur had great empathy for the fact that I had family there," Mrs. Bernstein said in a later reminiscence on the same conversation. "And he wanted to honor that, to honor me. Yes, he understood that I knew my way around and that I knew people there I could call on for support. But really it was his recognition of how much I *cared* about this, and how much it meant to me personally. I was very moved by that. The truth is, we always had enormous respect for one another, and that was an expression of his respect for me, which meant a lot to me."

It was also an expression of total commitment to the idea—and to the mountain of effort and money it would entail. When Mr. Fried said, "Let's *do* it," he meant it literally. He did not just mean, "Let's *fund* it." With Mrs. Bernstein's agreement, the foundation promptly set out to buy a piece of real estate, renovate its buildings, equip them, and provide an attractive, modern learning environment where Mr. Alper and Ms. Pechner could create and grow their school and parents would feel drawn to enroll their children.

Over the next few months, the Keshet trustees scoured the Bay Area looking for a suitable site. They examined several institutional and commercial possibilities, including an opportunity to join forces with people organizing a high school in the South Bay. But that proved to be too far away from San Francisco to serve most of its Jewish families. At another point, they took an interest in the former site of the Golden Gate Baptist Seminary in Mill Valley, a 148-acre former Marin County dairy farm where the newly formed United Nations had once sought to build its headquarters. The site enjoyed spectacular views of the San Francisco skyline to its south, but it was huge, expensive, and, like the South Bay site, too far from the region's center.

At last they came upon the California College of Podiatric Medicine, which was moving out of a small cluster of buildings on Scott Street in San Francisco's Western Addition. It was far from a perfect site—it was not beautiful like the Baptist seminary, nor was it ideally situated for public transportation. The parcel contained some older structures besides the 1970s-era main building and its parking garage. Some outlying buildings would need to be demolished, and at least one, a multi-wing hospital, would require environmental remediation. The podiatric college had bought the land from the San Francisco Redevelopment Authority, which limited its market potential, given that redevelopment rules at the time required it to be used for some kind of public benefit (educational institutions were acceptable). But despite its challenges, the property was affordable and, with the right amount of loving care, clearly had the potential to become an impressive campus. Keren Keshet created a subsidiary through which it bought the college in August 2001 for $27.1 million. Renovation would cost nearly $11 million more.

This was a prime example of Keren Keshet's unusual method of operating. Another foundation might have first declared a strategic interest in Jewish secondary education, then commissioned a study of high school capacity in the five largest U.S. Jewish communities, and then maybe picked one that had the greatest need and the ripest mix of educational and financial assets. Or it might have discovered a star educator with an innovative master plan for a new Jewish school and joined a list of funders ready to back the venture. Or it might have first demanded a business plan and cost-benefit analysis to gauge the "social return" on any proposed grant. Instead, Keshet responded to a spontaneous appeal from Jewish families who wanted a Jewish education for their children, and, relying on Mrs. Bernstein's firsthand knowledge of the Bay Area, plunged in. It was a case of an opportunity to do good that crossed their paths at a propitious moment, when they had more than enough money to bring their vision to life. And that was reason enough to proceed.

Sure enough, the property turned out to be every bit as challenging as it seemed when the foundation trustees first saw it, and more so. Richard Springwater, who served as the project's developer under contract with Keren Keshet, had provided the original due-diligence assessment of the site before the purchase, oversaw the planning and design, and managed the complex negotiations with the podiatrists and the redevelopment agency all the way through to closing. So he knew well the difficulties he was about to face, beginning with demolition and environmental remediation on the hospital and other buildings, which needed to be cleared away to make space for what would become the high school's courtyard and surrounding land-scaping.

And then there was the matter of the "cadaver room."

"In the due diligence process," Mr. Springwater recalled, "you've got a roster of specialist consultants you have to bring in, depending on the type of property, and in this case that included a bioremediation consultant, who searches for biological contaminants. And the main location for those was in the podiatric hospital building, where part of the demo would be the removal of the cadaver room. In other places, they found mercury in the drains and other things we would have to deal with. But the cadaver room was something else altogether. It was pretty grim. Human remains. It was really disgusting; there's no other word for it."

The actual cadavers were gone, mercifully. But remnants of body parts and bodily fluids were everywhere, the residue of years of desultory cleaning and sanitary procedures. At one early point in the project, the bioremediation team—professionals who spend much of their time in unhealthy and unsavory conditions—walked off the job in revulsion. The cleanup "did get done eventually," Mr. Springwater continued. "But it was one of those things you don't have to deal with when you acquire an office building."

The podiatric school's main classroom building, a two-story, L-shaped, tilt-up concrete structure of little architectural distinction, would become the high school. But first, its labs and lecture halls would need to be reconfigured to create a variety of learning spaces for younger students. Moreover, to satisfy the trustees' desire for a striking, enticing physical presence, it would have to undergo an aesthetic makeover, turning a plain, unimaginative building into a sleek, minimalist one. But long before all of that could be completed, students would need to be moving in quickly. In the time between the school's first proposal and the purchase of the building, more than two years had elapsed. The fledgling high school, still operating in the synagogue's makeshift classrooms in Tiburon, was about to enroll a sophomore class and needed a larger, permanent home as soon as possible.

The first phase of work, beginning in early 2002, would renovate a little over half of the 62,000-square-foot podiatry building, and it would have to be done by the start of the school year. The rest of the structure would remain untouched until the next summer. A second phase, adding new classroom and office space in a north wing, would be completed by 2004, and the podiatrists' auditorium would be converted into a fully equipped, 200-seat performing arts theater two years after that. The building came to life little by little, as the school welcomed an additional class each year until it encompassed grades 9 through 12.

Transforming a drab medical complex into a vibrant, inviting high school campus was a task that combined imagination, technical skill, and a certain amount of love. Mr. Fried, in particular, had made a specialty of using philanthropic resources to create distinguished buildings that represented lofty values, and he drew great personal satisfaction from them. Among other things, his Rothschild Foundation grants to build the Israeli Supreme Court building were a highlight of his charitable career. Going far beyond the boundaries of ordinary grantmaking, Mr. Fried had worked closely throughout the project with its architect and builders, as well as with members of the Supreme Court, to ensure that the building would be a fitting monument to Israel's system of justice.

Now, to create the high school, he and Mrs. Bernstein drew on a comparable sense of mission. Even small things drew their careful scrutiny. For instance, foreseeing (correctly) that the school would one day field a competitive varsity basketball team, they insisted on up-market, glass backstops for the outdoor nets. On a grander scale, they envisioned what Mr. Fried called "a really magnificent school yard"—an idea partly dictated by the aesthetic demands of the site (a plain concrete classroom building needed elegant surroundings to make it feel warmer and more distinguished). But just as important, the vision was based on the trustees' belief that the foundation was giving birth to something important and enduring for the Jewish community. They wanted the property to have an appearance worthy of its mission.

So when the project's landscape architect, Kevin Conger, was beginning to plan the "really magnificent school yard," one of his first challenges was how to handle an area designated for paving in a way that would look impressive without running up a huge cost. He was combing through catalogues of stone, seeking options with the right combination of beauty and affordability. But then Mr. Fried thought of an alternative—an idea that had at least as much to do with heart and soul as with budget.

At that moment, in his role as chairman of AVI CHAI, Mr. Fried was overseeing yet another of his great philanthropic building projects: the creation of a grand cultural center in Jerusalem, among the last requests of the late Mr. Bernstein, to be known as Beit AVI CHAI. Given its location in the middle of Jerusalem, where parking is scarce, the project needed a deep underground parking garage, and that meant excavating tons of high-grade limestone. The stone would then be available as building material. The century-old Israeli firm quarrying the site, A. Gribelsky and Son, praised the "Jerusalem Gold" that its crews were removing from the Beit AVI CHAI site as "supreme quality" in "inviting warm tones." Why shouldn't San Francisco's new Jewish high school boast a courtyard of such impressive material literally rooted in the heart of Jerusalem?

Within a matter of weeks, from the excavation site on King George Street in Jerusalem, the Gribelsky company began cutting and hauling enough limestone, sized to suit Mr. Conger's design, to fill two 20-foot shipping containers. When the containers arrived from Israel at the Port of Oakland, trucks then took the contents across the Bay to Scott Street, where a team of subcontractors was ready to lay them.

"It's a sweet story," project manager Richard Springwater said, remembering Mr. Fried's original inspiration. "Whenever I take people on a tour, I tell them that the foundation that built this high school used the ground under its own headquarters building in Jerusalem to quarry the pavers that you're now standing on. I hope the students continue to be fully aware of where those pavers come from. It's a wonderful thing."

Mr. Fried's "Let's do it" had constituted a bold philanthropic leap, an embrace of an enormous challenge of institution-building with no sure sign of support from the city's Jewish establishment. Still, although they were prepared to be the principal backers of a sizable new institution, the Keshet trustees were not, at that point, expecting to pay the entire cost by themselves. Ms. Pechner's and Mr. Alper's vision struck them as a tantalizing opportunity, and they imagined that others in the area's pantheon of Jewish philanthropy, surveying what Mr. Fried called a "desert of Jewish secondary education," would eventually feel the same way. Future stages of work might spark someone's imagination, and some aspects of the building—the auditorium, for instance—could provide naming opportunities for a major contributor. (Keren Keshet itself never sought to put its name on anything.) The uniqueness of the project, its timeliness, and the opportunity to leave a lasting legacy benefiting many thousands of Jewish kids all seemed like an ideal proposition for soliciting major donations.

With that hope of major new funding in mind, the foundation had treated the purchase of the Scott Street property as a kind of challenge grant for the new school and its community: Raise $20 million over the next five years, and we will turn over the land and buildings as a gift. Here, too, was a prime naming opportunity for a major donor. "We'll see how San Francisco rises to the occasion," Mrs. Bernstein told the Jewish News of Northern California in a moment of optimism. "We don't see the high school as just a building with students in it. We see it as an opportunity for the next generation of leaders in San Francisco."[2]

In 2002, Keren Keshet underwrote a detailed fundraising plan for the school, designed by the Greenwood Company, a national consultancy specializing in big-donor campaigns. Greenwood outlined a two-phase strategy in which the school would recruit prominent Jewish philanthropists for its board and campaign committees and would begin appealing to the broader community, starting with the Jewish Federation. A list of prospective donors would be compiled with Greenwood's help, with priority assigned to those most likely to be lead donors—people whose sizable early donations and communal prominence would inspire others to climb on board. At the same time, a team of school leaders would be trained in techniques for pursuing major gifts and would be supplied with publications, videos, and core messages to fuel their efforts. In a second phase, from mid-2003 to the start of the 2004-05 school year, a stream of face-to-face solicitations would take place, with one team targeting the top 100 prospects and another focusing on the lower tier.

In the meantime, Keren Keshet would underwrite a substantial share of the school's ongoing expenses, including providing free tuition for two years for all students in the first three classes. In the trustees' view, the key to the school's success would be to attract a large and outstanding cadre of students, thus amassing a reputation as a desirable community full of bright classmates. San Francisco is fertile ground for elite high schools, and many gifted graduates of Jewish lower schools were moving on to one of these secular private schools—or even, in some cases, to Catholic parochial schools—after 8th grade. Wouldn't they prefer a Jewish alternative if it offered comparable quality? The free tuition would lay the groundwork by demonstrating that possibility.

Thereafter, the foundation would for decades continue providing merit-based scholarships for the best students and means-based scholarships for the needier families. But giving the entire school a free ride for the first two years was yet another extraordinary philanthropic gesture: essentially a market-making tactic designed to position the Jewish Community High School of the Bay as a prime destination for families seeking the best possible secondary education in a Jewish environment.

Of course, even with guaranteed tuition for two years, operating the school would be an expensive prospect, with costs that were still mounting. So to help its board meet the $20 million challenge, and to jump-start the Greenwood Company's campaign plan, the Keshet trustees reached out to one of Mr. Fried's former partners at Lehman Brothers, who was now a prominent financier and philanthropist in the Bay Area. He agreed to gather a dozen or so major donors to explore the possibilities and to envision what the school could become with sufficient backing. Expecting a warm reception, or at least a stirring of interest, Mr. Fried and Mrs. Bernstein headed to San Francisco to make their pitch.

It was a near-total failure. "They basically said, 'Don't do it. Don't come here,'" Mrs. Bernstein recalled, still stinging from the cold reception after nearly 20 years. "They said they weren't interested in seeing a Jewish community high school in San Francisco, and they meant it. They may have thought that we were going to walk away from it at some point and leave them to carry the full expense, and they didn't want the responsibility. I don't know. But for whatever reason, the answer was 'No, thanks.'"

Stunned and disappointed, the two trustees returned to New York. Some additional contributions did come forth through the fundraising campaign designed by Greenwood, including from Mr. Alper, Ms. Pechner, and their families, as well as a few other individual donors. Philanthropist Bruce Dolan gave $1 million and the new courtyard was named for him. But these contributions never collectively approached the original challenge amount, nor did the Jewish Community Federation ever adopt the high school as a fixture of its annual giving.

Over the years, Mr. Fried and Mrs. Bernstein continued their outreach to major donors in hopes of finding at least one or two partners with whom to share the care and feeding of the young high school. But time after time, they learned that prospective donors had interests of their own and would consider helping Keren Keshet only if Keren Keshet in turn supported some of their causes. This mutual back-scratching, which Mr. Fried routinely dismisses with the Hebrew expression *sh'mor li, v'eshmor l'cha* (roughly: "you look out for me, and I'll look out for you") rarely leads to wise philanthropy, in their view. Worse, it bears no relationship to the essential merits of the case they were trying to make. They were not asking other funders to do them a favor, but to take a share in nurturing something of demonstrable communal value, filling a giant, obvious gap in local Jewish life.

Another time, the response from an exceptionally wealthy San Franciscan, known for generous philanthropy, seemed on the verge of becoming exactly the partnership Mrs. Bernstein and Mr. Fried were hoping for. The prospective donor seemed to understand the school's importance and plainly had the means to help it grow in both size and quality. Then came the catch: In exchange for a sizable donation, Keren Keshet would have to grant the school full ownership of the property. As the donor saw it, this would allow administrators to borrow against the real estate, thus making funds available immediately, even as additional money was being raised. But from the foundation's perspective, it was a deal-breaker. Keren Keshet would be pleased to extend the current lease and to keep it rent-free for at least another ten years, Mrs. Bernstein wrote, in an attempt to negotiate a middle ground. But "we will not transfer title to the property to the JCHS. Please understand that, after purchasing the school, renovating it, and granting large sums to maintain it for almost 20 years, we consider it a valuable asset of our Foundation." The deal was off— although the donor did make a much smaller contribution later, without receiving any real estate in return.

But these abortive efforts to recruit a mega-donor were rare and fleeting. As far back as that initial meeting with the Olympians of Bay Area Jewish philanthropy, it had become clear that the school would essentially be a Keren Keshet venture, at least until it could gather enough steam to roll forth on its own. Between 2001 and 2013, annual foundation grants to the Jewish Community High School of the Bay ran between $2 million and $3 million a year, usually closer to the higher figure. The sums dropped slightly for the next three years, closer to $1.5 million annually through 2016, for a total of more than $40 million over 20 years. That figure does not include the costs of owning and maintaining the property, which amounted to another $800,000 a year, on average, in the high school's first two decades.

Mr. Fried's "Let's do it" had become, "Let's do it mostly alone."

———————

If local philanthropy was not going to pour forth to the Jewish Community High School, then attracting a sizable enrollment—especially of paying students—would become all the more urgent. Here, too, the results never matched the trustees' early hopes, though enrollment figures have climbed slowly but steadily over the years. Bringing in more students was a task that the leaders of the school and of the foundation shared, but they never viewed it in quite the same light. For Mrs. Bernstein in particular, the main challenge, after ensuring academic quality and solid Jewish content, was essentially one of marketing. The school was providing an excellent education in both Jewish and general studies, in a well-equipped, modern, and attractive environment (Mrs. Bernstein personally chose many of the design elements).

Its mission was to deepen the Jewish knowledge and identity of the community's next generations. This, she believed, called for aggressive, smart promotion. And Keren Keshet was prepared to fund such an effort, with top-ranked marketing consultants, with nationally known Jewish personalities speaking at the school, and with continued outreach to Jewish communal leaders, even if they were still reluctant to open their wallets. Because San Francisco had never before had a Jewish high school like this one—serious about deep Jewish learning, including Hebrew language, but also pluralistic and non-dogmatic, and equally serious about secular studies—the word would need to be spread. Families who feared that a "Jewish" high school could either be too insistently religious or not academically ambitious enough needed to be drawn in to see the appealing reality of this new institution.

The world of school leadership, however, tends to be more reticent. Many educators are wary of razzle-dazzle and believe that a school's reputation is best served by projecting a dignified, scholarly demeanor—in essence, emphasizing gravitas over pizzazz. Whether for this reason or others, the school's board and administrative leaders seemed reluctant to embrace Mrs. Bernstein's repeated offers of help with marketing, visiting celebrities, and other means of promotion. Nonetheless, Keren Keshet did pay for, and persuade the school to accept, one year of advice from BlueStarPR, a firm that specializes in promoting positive perceptions of Israel and thus has extensive experience in the Jewish communal world. The choice was a careful one: BlueStar is not a slick, Madison Avenue firm, but one with a sizable clientele in the realm of Jewish education, a close working relationship with the Jewish press, and a focus on attracting positive media and changing perceptions, not on hard salesmanship.

During its year at the Jewish Community High School of the Bay, BlueStar developed promotional events and opportunities around the school's successful boys' basketball team, including an event for families of Jewish middle-school students at a Golden State Warriors game. The firm pitched articles about the school to local media, helped revamp the school's website and graphic identity, expanded its database of prospective enrollees and their families, and helped energize the school's Parents' Association. It blanketed the San Francisco Jewish Film Festival with Jewish Community High School ads and sponsorships. It sought to work with school leaders to redesign the building's entryway, upgrade the newsletter for families, bolster other external and internal communications, and train staff in various marketing techniques.[3]

Despite an enthusiastic reception from students and families, and from at least some faculty members, BlueStar reported at the end of the year that "in the end, we were unable to motivate the Senior Staff to bring about lasting change." Most of the firm's accomplishments turned out to be one-offs. A proposed school newspaper, for example, was fully developed but went nowhere. ("A draft edition in a fairly advanced state of preparation was delivered to admissions for perusal and comments," the firm reported at the end of its year of effort, "but no response, either negative or positive, was ever forthcoming.") A professionally produced video showcasing the school and spotlighting some of its students and faculty was completed but never distributed. (Short videos narrated by students, spotlighting various features of the school, were produced many years later and posted prominently on its website.) A planned student performance at an annual public event honoring Israel, which took BlueStar some effort to negotiate, was canceled "due to lack of enthusiasm from faculty and staff, despite the prominence and attention it would have received."

It was clear, from these experiences, that pressuring the school into marketing efforts that were plainly outside its comfort zone was little more than a burden on the school and a waste of money for Keren Keshet. The administration did add a senior position for what it called a director of advancement, encompassing marketing, fundraising, and external relations, but it didn't embrace most of the outreach measures that BlueStar had tried to launch. The foundation didn't press the matter further.[4]

It did, however, continue to seek new ways of raising Jewish families' awareness of the high school, both by outreach to students enrolled in Jewish elementary and middle schools and by bringing Jewish San Franciscans into the high school building. One imaginative effort started as a partnership with Brandeis-Hillel Day School, a Jewish K-8 school in San Francisco's Park Merced neighborhood. Beginning in 2006, Keren Keshet offered students at Brandeis a scholarship grant of $500 for every year they were enrolled there, usable toward tuition at the Jewish Community High School. The money would be in addition to other financial aid the student might receive, whether based on merit or need. It was a win-win for both schools: The scholarship provided an incentive both for students to remain at Brandeis and then to continue their Jewish education at the high school. By year's end, four other Bay Area day schools had signed on, thus covering nearly every school from which a student might enter the Jewish Community High School. To keep the feeder system lubricated, Keren Keshet also made direct annual grants to several of the schools to support their general operations.

Another effort to boost the high school's visibility involved the Bay Area Jewish library. From the beginning, Mr. Fried and Mrs. Bernstein were determined that the school would have an outstanding library, given the important role books and reading played in Zalman Bernstein's life and philanthropy. But they felt no need to create a new school library from scratch—in fact, there was good reason not to do so. The Jewish Community Library of San Francisco was then housed in cramped and uninviting quarters in an area where parking could be difficult. Moving the library to the new high school campus would be another win-win proposition: The library would get larger, more comfortable, modern quarters, and could share parking in the former podiatry school's garage, which had more than enough spaces. The school would get not only a complete, richly stocked Jewish library, but a way of connecting to the wider Jewish community as well. In addition to welcoming regular patrons day after day, the library also hosts many special programs and events throughout the year. The trustees hoped this stream of visitors would get a good look at the school, and the school would be able to reach out to them.

"We helped the library start a Sunday morning program for children there," Mrs. Bernstein pointed out, in addition to a stream of foundation grants for other library activities. "It was all in the hope that the community would come to the building, see our high school, recognize what a great place it is, and maybe send their children there." The foundation paid to relocate the library and enrich its collection. It also guaranteed that, if the new location didn't work out, the foundation would pay to re-house the library elsewhere. Fifteen years later, the library remains happily ensconced on the high school campus.

And the result has been positive for both institutions, up to a point. People do routinely come to the campus to visit the library; they park in the garage and enjoy pleasant surroundings and security largely provided by the high school. Visitors get a look at the campus, and some library programs have been beneficial to the school's students and faculty. But the hoped-for partnership between the two institutions, with jointly sponsored programs and extensive school-community interaction, never really jelled. Even as this is written, in 2021, the library's web site makes no mention of the high school. It gives its location merely by the street address, with no suggestion that another important Jewish community institution shares the premises.

"Five or six or seven years after the school was built," Mrs. Bernstein lamented, "I could still sit at a dinner [for a Jewish communal organization], and people at the table wouldn't even know there's a high school there. That's been part of the frustration."

Even as renovations on the building were progressing, the high school's board and staff were becoming concerned about some important features that the new facility would lack—things that, they believed, would make a big difference in their ability to recruit more students. Chief among these was a gym, and nearly as important was a high-tech center for teaching science, technology, engineering, and math, the so-called STEM disciplines. The foundation was then in the process of purchasing all the remaining property on the city block bounded by Scott, Ellis, Pierce, and Eddy Streets, including a small strip that was owned, as the school site had been, by San Francisco's Redevelopment Agency. Given that this additional parcel would be subject to the same rules as the school property, requiring it to be used for some public benefit, perhaps it could become the home of a new gym and STEM center for the high school.

The pleas from high school leaders reminded Mr. Fried of characters from the Wizard of Oz: "If I only had a gym!" Many years later, he still chuckled about the persistence of the board and administrators in making the case for the additional facilities. But he and Mrs. Bernstein took the proposition more than seriously at the time. Other private schools in the area had gyms, and a STEM center would be a big competitive asset in San Francisco's ubiquitous tech sector. For all its uneasiness about aggressive marketing, the school's leaders clearly grasped the reputational advantages these new facilities would bring, and they envisioned a swell of additional enrollments as a consequence.

Alas, it was not to be. The trustees managed to purchase the strip from the Redevelopment Agency, alongside a separate acquisition of some apartment buildings at the corner of Ellis and Pierce. Together, these purchases, combined with the school, library, and parking garage, completed the foundation's ownership of the whole block. Redevelopment officials required that some construction take place on its parcel very quickly, so the foundation commissioned a design for the gym/STEM building and poured a foundation. That was enough to satisfy the city that the strip would not be put to an ineligible use.

But there the project halted. By the time the footings were being poured in the excavated strip, the chances that the school would meet its $20 million fundraising target had shrunk nearly to zero. An expected donor for the gym fell ill and was no longer able to fulfill his funding pledge. Nor was enrollment matching projections or supplying anywhere near the hoped-for number of students able to pay full tuition. Burdening the school with yet another building that it would not be able to maintain seemed foolish. As it was, Keren Keshet was paying the full cost of maintaining the existing structures, and the hope that this cost would someday be transferred to the school was receding farther and farther into the future. Now was not the time to dig the money pit any deeper.

Nor did the newly acquired apartment buildings seem as promising an asset for the school as they did at the time the foundation decided to buy them. At first, while optimism still ran high, Mr. Fried and Mrs. Bernstein envisioned someday creating a boarding school, effectively converting some of the apartment space into dormitories. Later, they considered using some or all of the apartments as offices, faculty housing, or both. But these ideas faded in much the same way that the gym building did: Financial momentum would need to pick up dramatically for any such prospects to become feasible. As this is written, more than 15 years after the purchase, neither the gym parcel nor the apartment complex has developed into anything beyond what it was originally, and no plans have been made to do anything new with them.

––––––––

When Keren Keshet first announced that it was buying property for the Jewish Community High School, the local media noted that the converted podiatry college had enough space, in theory, for as many as 1,000 students. The school's headmaster at the time made clear that the official projections were far more modest than that: Enrollment would be no greater than 400.[5]

The period of such heady expectations wasn't long. Within the first year, the target dropped to 240 students, but even that number soon proved unrealistic in the near term. Three years after it opened, the school had fewer than 60 students. That same year, Keren Keshet contributed $2.3 million, prompting Mr. Fried to note that it was paying roughly $42,000 per student per year in operating costs alone, not counting the cost of maintaining the property or continuing renovations to the building. The following year, with only a slight increase in enrollment and no appreciable rise in the number paying full tuition, the foundation's infusion rose to $3.4 million. The trustees were beginning to question the return on their investment.

By this time, the foundation had added a new chief financial officer, Yehuda Novick, to its staff. Unlike CFOs in most foundations, Mr. Novick served both as the internal manager of the institution's own resources and as a source of financial expertise for grantees. In cases where the foundation's investment in an organization was large and complex, or where the grantee's finances were precarious, he effectively became part of the program team, working alongside Linda Sakacs and Evan Feinsilver to keep tabs on a project's economics.

Mr. Novick had come to Keren Keshet through family connections—

his brother Azriel was the CFO of AVI CHAI—after a Wall Street career that had included stints at Arthur Andersen, JPMorgan, Bankers Trust, and Merrill Lynch. When he and his family started planning to make Aliyah, the prospect of following his brother into philanthropy—and particularly a philanthropy with bases in both Israel and New York—took on particular appeal. The invitation from Mr. Fried and Mrs. Bernstein was almost perfectly timed. He started at Keren Keshet in 2003.

At that point, it was already apparent that the foundation's high school project was going to need what Mr. Novick called "financial TLC." The closer he looked at its fiscal management, the less confident he felt—not because of any malfeasance, but because the administration routinely operated with too little information, hardly any ability to forecast, and only the shortest-term planning. Targets for enrollment, fundraising, and expenses all bore a taint of wishful thinking. While educational quality and content were steadily rising, and the faculty and staff were earning high marks for doing their most important job—delivering a topnotch education—Mr. Novick concluded that the non-academic side of the enterprise was suffering. He began a series of regular visits to San Francisco, often with Mrs. Sakacs, Mrs. Bernstein, or both, to review the books, confer with the school's CFO, assemble more complete information, and train a keener eye on ways to rein in spending.

At first, school administrators tried to assure him that the current problems were temporary, and that big leaps in student recruitment and fundraising were just over the horizon. "Maybe that's true," he told them, "but those are factors that are not completely in your control. What you have in your control are things like class sizes, payroll, tuition, the percentage of the budget that goes to financial aid. Those are all things you can change." On many of these issues, the field of

Jewish day school education had abundant data for comparison, which Mr. Novick helped school leaders to assemble and analyze. Better data and better financial management helped steady the ship in some ways, though the seas remained rough.

The years of diagnosing and remedying problems was slow and not always amicable. One early head of the school pointedly demanded to know how long the foundation intended to stay involved in his budgeting—a query that drew a predictably terse response: as long as the budget depends mostly on us.

But for the most part, the partnership between Mr. Novick and his counterparts at the high school proceeded smoothly, with steadily rising confidence on both sides. The issues they had to tackle, however, were thorny, and in many cases they struggled to settle on firm solutions. One example was the level of tuition. In 2006, Mrs. Bernstein noted that the full annual cost of attending the Jewish Community High School had risen to twice as high as at two local Catholic schools. Administrators argued that the increase was necessary to close budget gaps, but Mrs. Bernstein worried that some Jewish families might feel compelled to enroll their children in Catholic schools. A year later, conversely, school leaders contemplated a sharp *reduction* in tuition, speculating that a more attractive price might bring in a much larger number of paying students. That idea never took off; instead, tuition went up by 4 percent for the following school year.

By then, enrollment had risen to 157 students—significant growth, but still 5 percent below that year's target, and nearly 35 percent below even the moderate target of 240 that had been set when the school was created. The failure to reach the desired enrollment contributed to an emergency grant request to Keren Keshet in 2008 of nearly $500,000. For Mr. Novick and the trustees—and, painfully, for school officials as well—it was clear that the time for serious cost-cutting had come. Mr. Fried cautioned that the foundation should "not interject itself into the [cost-saving] process at this time," but should leave the particulars of what would be cut, and by how much, up to the school's leaders. Nonetheless, Mr. Novick and Mrs. Sakacs would monitor the process closely and advise if asked.

At this point, the long-deferred expectation that the school would gradually wean itself from Keren Keshet's operating grants and would eventually begin paying for building maintenance was also made official. The school was given a schedule of diminishing annual grants and a deadline for assuming property maintenance costs by 2017. Difficult cuts in personnel soon followed, even as the search for more economies continued.

Efforts at boosting enrollment and fundraising also accelerated at this point, driven in part by the arrival of a relatively new, more business-minded head of school. Rabbi Howard Ruben, previously of Cleveland, Ohio, took the reins in 2008 and quickly began making adjustments. His selection had been the result of a national search, after a succession of brief and temporary appointments that had given the school three headmasters in five years. Rabbi Ruben, who remains on the job as this is written, introduced a long period of stability and growing confidence from Keren Keshet that the school was now in the capable hands of not only a skilled educator but a prudent manager. Soon after he arrived, board membership was enlarged to bring on more Bay Area philanthropists and Jewish community leaders, and outreach to students in Jewish elementary and middle schools intensified. By 2010, the percentage of students paying full tuition had risen—a crucial revenue goal—but enrollment growth was leveling off.

The desire for a rising enrollment had long been in tension with one of the foundation's fundamental goals for creating a Jewish high school: a rigorous Judaic education, including a mastery of Hebrew. The requirement of a first-rate Jewish education was spelled out in the lease from Keren Keshet by which the high school occupied the property on Scott Street. To be sure, families who choose a Jewish education share that goal, up to a point, and measure a school partly with the quality of its Jewishness in mind. Demonstrating real excellence in these subjects can therefore have some marketing benefits, provided the school is at least equally outstanding in other subjects that are more important to university admissions offices.

But beyond a certain point, time devoted to Jewish studies and the pursuit of fluency in Hebrew can sometimes backfire. Some students, even if they value a solid knowledge of their history and culture, would prefer to master more widely spoken languages. They might prefer to spend more of their school day on math or technology. In Palo Alto, 30 miles south of San Francisco, Kehillah Jewish High School saw a jump in its enrollment when it shrunk its Hebrew language curriculum to require just one year of Hebrew basics. Reluctantly, but seeing little alternative, the Jewish Community High School of the Bay instituted some trimming of its own Jewish curriculum, while still laboring to stay faithful to its founding mission and the foundation-imposed terms of its property lease.

Despite all these efforts, and with enrollments projected at a then-record high of 180, the school still faced a $300,000 deficit for the 2012–13 academic year. Matters only grew worse when the number of entering freshmen able to pay full tuition turned out to be barely half what was expected. At this point, just over half the money technically classified as tuition was actually paid by students and their families. The rest came from philanthropy—mostly Keren Keshet. A year later, the deficit had swollen to $950,000 and the percentage of students paying full tuition had fallen to 33. These figures improved only slightly in the next five years.

To make matters even more dire, the schedule of diminishing foundation grants, which had originally been set forth in 2009, was now approaching its final four years. By that schedule, the operating support would end in the 2016–17, after which the school would still pay no rent, but it would have to cover all its own operating costs and pay for security and maintenance on the property. By now, of course, this was obviously unrealistic, and in early 2014, Keren Keshet formally extended the deadline to the 2020–21 school year. But even that relaxed schedule placed the school's leadership under enormous pressure. Even Mr. Novick acknowledged that it was difficult to foresee how the goal would be met without a significant outpouring of local philanthropy.

At the start of 2020, just short of the school's 18th birthday, the chairman of its board informed Mrs. Bernstein that he and his colleagues were not yet certain that they would be able to admit a new freshman class in September. The foundation responded with yet another emergency grant, and a new class was, in fact, admitted. Other donors subsequently came forward to pave the way to a subsequent academic year. But Mr. Fried and Mrs. Bernstein discouraged any further discussion of ongoing "emergency" grants, noting what they had written in a 2015 letter: "It has always been the hope, never more than now, that the Bay Area Jewish community will rally to the needs of the *Jewish Community* High School" (emphasis in the original). Five years later, they are adhering to that position: As they see it, the time for Keren Keshet to step back and for the Bay Area Jewish leadership to take over has arrived.

By 2021, "Let's do it" was rapidly becoming, "We did what we could."

The financial horizon hasn't been without bright spots. For the 2020–21 academic year, fundraising reached $2.1 million, considerably more than had seemed possible just a few years earlier. During the first year of the Covid pandemic, with reduced expenses and assistance from the federal Paycheck Protection Program, the high school actually ran a budget surplus of $1.2 million. With students returning to in-person learning the following year, the red ink has returned, with an $800,000 projected deficit. But that is accounted for in large part by the costs of site maintenance, which Keren Keshet had previously been paying and the school has now absorbed.

New donors continue to materialize, including a small but symbolically important grant of $100,000 from the Chan-Zuckerberg Initiative, the foundation of Facebook founder Mark Zuckerberg and his wife, the physician Priscilla Chan. And major donors have sustained or increased their support, including the Jim Joseph Foundation, among other bold-face names in the Bay Area Jewish community.

Finances aside, it is essential to note that, for two decades, the school has achieved its primary, overarching goal: to equip generations of young Jewish students with an outstanding, well-rounded education steeped in Jewish learning, scripture, traditions, spirituality, and solidarity. A comprehensive 2008 evaluation of the Jewish Community High School by the nonprofit research firm Education Matters, based in Cambridge, Mass., found it to be "a vibrant, high-quality day school" that is "worthy of the community's continuing commitment." Noting the tenuousness of that communal commitment, the evaluators nonetheless praised the founders and donors for establishing a pluralistic Jewish high school "where none had existed before, in a community that is not quite sure where it stands with respect to religious education."[6] In short, the authors credited the school with both offering a top-quality learning experience and making a powerful, living case to the San Francisco Jewish establishment for the importance of Jewish education in grades 9–12.

In a detailed survey of general academic content, the evaluation commended "a strong faculty, a group of teachers dedicated to the school, its students, and its mission." Even after noting "the changing and interim leadership that has characterized the school in its first years,"[7] the study found a solid and consistent commitment to educational standards and responsiveness to individual student needs, even when that resulted in some expensive and administratively difficult arrangements, like extremely small class sizes in some cases, or multiple levels of instruction in various subjects.

On the Jewish Studies curriculum, a topic of particular importance to Keren Keshet, evaluators found "an excellent set of rigorous and engaging courses" tailored for students with differing degrees of prior Jewish education, including those with little or none.[8] They noted that the school was easing some Jewish studies requirements and introducing more individual choice into the content of each student's Jewish education. While this might be taken, on the surface, as "weakening" the curriculum, evaluators viewed it as an effective "strategy for dealing with more students."[9] In other words, given the school's urgent need to increase enrollment, adjusting the curriculum to the likely diversity of larger and larger incoming classes was essential. The changes were not only necessary, but an effective way to deliver as much Jewish learning as possible to different kinds of students. In that respect, "the curricular visions being put in place represent a strengthening of the school's efforts to achieve its mission for Jewishly educating its students."[10]

The evaluators also looked closely at experiential Jewish learning—especially the daily options for tefillah and various extracurricular offerings aimed at deepening the experience of Jewish life. The report found that the school places a high value on "having students start each day with *holy time because this is what Jews do*" (emphasis in the original).[11] However, given the pluralistic character of the student body, JCHS provides students with multiple ways in which to experience holy time or tefillah" while ensuring "that it graduated students who were familiar with at least some aspects of siddur-based tefillah."[12]

Although the evaluation was primarily focused on the content of education at the high school, the researchers felt it important to add a note about the building and Keren Keshet's unstinting support for the material necessities of teaching and learning. "We would be remiss," they wrote, "if we did not report teachers' appreciation for the beautiful facility in which they teach and the availability of all the supplies and equipment they need. For many teachers, especially those that worked in urban or less-well-to-do schools prior to joining the JCHS faculty, not having to scrounge for materials or pay for them out of their own pockets is a welcome change."[13]

————

Mrs. Bernstein and Mr. Fried found the evaluation results reassuring, but they also believed that the real measure of success should lie in the *outcomes* of a Jewish Community High School education. It was good to know that the inputs—teaching, school leadership, extracurricular enrichment, an elevating environment for learning—largely met their expectations. But what mattered most to them was the Jewish lives of the students *after* they graduated. So even as the school-based evaluation was under way, they reached out in early 2008 to sociologist Steven M. Cohen, who was then Research Professor of Jewish Social Policy at the Hebrew Union College—Jewish

Institute of Religion, and one of the foremost scholars of American Jewish life.

The following year, at their behest, Dr. Cohen launched a decade-long research project to find out, as he put it, "To what extent are the alumni of Jewish Community High School of the Bay engaged in Jewish life—and in what ways?[14] He conducted nearly annual online surveys, plus a set of one-on-one interviews, to assemble an extended picture of how Judaism—and more specifically, a Jewish secondary education—influenced these young people's lives. He asked them about a list of 14 activities, experiences, and feelings that constitute Jewish living, including observance of holidays and rituals, prayer, text study, Jewish friendships and marriage, attachment to Israel, and feelings of belonging to and identifying with the Jewish people. As a comparison group, Dr. Cohen drew a demographically similar sample from the Pew Research Center's survey of Jewish Americans conducted in 2013.

As a point of departure, he took careful note of the peculiar environment in which the students would learn, graduate, and move on to adult lives. This would be a study not of young Jewish adults in New York, Miami, Boston, Chicago, or even nearby Los Angeles, where the tapestry of Jewish life is tightly woven, but in what Dr. Cohen described as a community that "scores relatively low on measures of Jewish engagement—in fact, lower than any other community in the world of comparable size or larger." San Francisco's Jewish population, he wrote, exhibits "low levels of ritual observance, communal affiliation, commitment, residential concentration, in-marriage, and related measures."

In setting out to support a high school, Mrs. Bernstein and Mr. Fried had taken this weak level of affiliation into account. But for all its risks, they had seen the lack of a strong Jewish core in the Bay Area as a prime reason *for* their project. Surely, they believed, a community with such weak centripetal forces would welcome a means of strengthening the Jewish awareness and identity of its children. By contrast, viewing the same reality, Dr. Cohen regarded the thin air of Judaism in the Bay Area as a major *impediment* not only to Jewish secondary study and the economic sustenance of a Jewish high school, but to the continuity of Jewish identity thereafter. "This Jewishly unengaged context," he wrote,

poses challenges to the school—or similar institutions—that seek to instill Jewish commitment on the part of young people. Religious instruction requires a 'plausibility structure'—social reinforcement for the distinctive ideas, beliefs, and behaviors of the religiously committed. But when few adults or age-peers exhibit religious or ethnocultural commitment, religious instruction doesn't 'make sense,' and seems counter-cultural at the very least.[15]

Nonetheless, as Mrs. Bernstein repeatedly argued, it would surely be better—for young Jews of the Bay Area, for the Jewish community, for Jewish communal institutions and leaders, and for the future of Judaism itself—to have an annual cohort of smart, Jewishly nurtured high school graduates entering society than not to have one. And Dr. Cohen's findings, though mixed, did affirm the importance of the Jewish Community High School education in reinforcing the lives of many alumni. Though graduating classes did not march out en masse into uniformly rich Jewish futures—an obviously fanciful expectation—many appear to have experienced a *more* Jewish transition to adulthood than they otherwise would have. And they seem, on average, to be more integrally attached to their Jewishness than is typical of the rest of the Jewish Bay Area—or even, in some ways, typical of Jewish young people elsewhere.

For example, nearly three-quarters of the graduates in Dr. Cohen's study feel "a strong sense of belonging to the Jewish people." More than 70 percent have "mostly Jewish friends." This last statistic stunned Dr. Cohen, who wrote, "While readily understandable for students attending a Jewish high school, the numbers for Jewish friends are 'off the charts' for American Jewish youth generally and for San Francisco Jewish teenagers especially."[16]

The study found significantly higher rates of synagogue membership among high school alumni, and an above-average rate of dating and in-marriage with Jewish partners. (This last fact was particularly intriguing, given that the graduates had roughly the same nonchalant attitude toward the *principle* of in-group marriage as the rest of the public: 63 percent of high school alumni said that people should marry whomever they please, regardless of religion.) Even among those who are intermarried or headed in that direction, the importance of raising Jewish children is still strongly held in many cases.[17]

Jewish Community High School alumni were not, as was once hoped, close to fluent in Hebrew. But they were far more at home with the language than the Pew Research Center comparison group, both in comprehension and ability to converse. Close to half of the high school graduates say they could carry on some form of conversation in Hebrew; only 18 percent of the Pew sample said they could do so.[18] Familiarity with Israel ran far above that in the Pew sample: 78 percent of the alumni had been to Israel twice or more (not counting those who moved there permanently). In the Pew sample, the comparable figure was 34 percent. Some 56 percent of the high school graduates described themselves as "very attached to Israel," compared with 34 percent in the Pew survey.[19]

Summing up, Dr. Cohen wrote, graduates of the Jewish Community High School "outscore the Pew comparison sample, sometimes by wide margins, on seven of the 14 indicators: Jewish friends, Seder participation, Shabbat candle-lighting, monthly service attendance, feeling that being Jewish is very important, feeling that religion is very important, and feeling very attached to Israel." On most other measures, including keeping a kosher home, fasting on Yom Kippur, belonging to a synagogue, and donating to Jewish charities, the two groups were roughly similar.[20]

On only one indicator of Jewish connectedness did the high school alumni score well below those in the Pew comparison group, but it is a telling one: The alumni were more than one-third less likely to believe in God. This is, on reflection, not especially surprising. The high school strives to be a pluralistic environment that welcomes non-religious Jewish students and their families and does not pressure them to change their beliefs. The school's influence thus can't be fairly measured by the religiosity of its graduates. Further, in ultra-secular San Francisco, it's likely that most other religious and ethnic groups would also report lower rates of religious belief than their counterparts nationwide.

Still, the fact that students' religious belief mirrors that of their neighbors and families better than that of their more-religious teachers and counselors—and that years of education in scripture and tradition apparently did little to perfume their emotional atmosphere with any fresh aroma of faith—points to a reality that Dr. Cohen raises frequently in his report: People's identity, beliefs, and cultural affinities derive much more from their families and social environment than from their schooling. This is true in general, and no less true among teenagers at the Jewish Community High School. Asked to name the major influences on their Jewish identity, "alumni most frequently cited their parents, childhood homes, and major annual holidays." Rabbis and grandparents came next on the list. Only when prompted, Dr. Cohen reports, did respondents mention teachers at the high school.[21]

The dependence of Jewish identity on the extent of Judaism in a student's family and social circle is a cautionary factor that runs through all of the report's findings, particularly those involving comparisons between graduates and the Pew survey respondents. The latter are drawn from the whole variegated landscape of American Jewry; the former come exclusively from young people whose families cared enough about Judaism to send them to a Jewish high school—in a city where even many of the local Jewish elders considered a Jewish high school unnecessary.

Dr. Cohen did go to great lengths to bridge some of this disparity between the two samples and to make them more comparable. Among other things, he "weighted the Pew sub-sample so as to increase the proportion who went to a Jewish day school," though not specifically to a Jewish high school.[22] He also re-weighted the sample "so that the children of the intermarried constituted the same fraction (16%) in the Pew group as among the JCHS alumni."[23] The result is still not quite an apples-to-apples comparison, he acknowledges, but with these adjustments, "the Pew sub-sample allows for deriving some sense in which JCHS graduates differ from their age peers across the United States."

Mrs. Bernstein and Mr. Fried are not much troubled by the imperfections in the comparison data. Nor are they concerned about the school's uncertain influence on religious belief, or even by the possibility that enrolling in the Jewish Community High School does more to reinforce other influences than to ignite Jewish fervency where none previously existed. Their purpose, as Mrs. Bernstein put it, was to "give families who want to raise knowledgeable and committed Jewish children a way of doing that, a way that we know correlates to affiliation later in life." One high school, whether its enrollment was 200 or 400 or even 1,000, was never going to turn the Bay Area into a kibbutz. But it could—and Dr. Cohen's research strongly suggests that it does—give substance and meaning to young Jewish lives, and a boost to committed Jewish parents, at a stage of life when young people are beginning to explore their identities and shape their worldview.

"And that's more than just enough," Mrs. Bernstein concluded. "That's something great."

———

For Keren Keshet, the Jewish Community High School of the Bay was never just a grantee, it was a labor of love. Particularly for Mrs. Bernstein, whose dreams for the school verged on the epic, the desire to see it blossom and thrive was in equal parts strategic, principled, and emotional. "I don't like to use this expression," she told an evaluator from Education Matters in 2008, "but in a way I'm a little bit like the mother here. And I'm certainly the person who has a great sense of pride of ownership. You know, it's our baby."[24]

Her meticulous, granular involvement in decisions about the school's furnishings, design, and atmosphere matched an almost equally devoted attention to its personnel and governance. As chair of its board for many years, she exerted enormous influence—in some cases, more than she knew—over major decisions by administrators and faculty leaders. Some of them chafed under the pressure from someone they regarded as loving, protective, and generous—but not qualified to run a school. The fact that she maintained an office in the building struck some in the administration as a subtle signal that "the mother" was watching.

This fear of constant surveillance was highly exaggerated and completely opposite to Mrs. Bernstein's intentions. But it had consequences. For example, the revolving door of headmasters in the school's early years, prior to the arrival of Rabbi Ruben, was wrongly, though widely, attributed to Mrs. Bernstein. Some people plainly believed that any sign of her displeasure instantly became a mandate to make a change. "The word was sort of out there," a board member told the evaluators, speaking about the periodic searches for new headmasters, "that if you come, you're going to have this extra governing entity to deal with."[25] Although the board member characterized this impression as "based on rumors that are really untrue," the rumors were not entirely baseless. "There were many times," Mrs. Bernstein conceded, "when I would do something without even discussing it" with the school's executives.[26]

As she became more aware of this dynamic, she started easing back from some of her feelings of "ownership," seeking to become more of a partner and resource for the high school's full-time leaders. She took steps to limit her interactions with faculty and staff to the realms of fundraising, public relations, and marketing. Even so, some administrators and board members continued to find her presence disquieting, according to interviews that Education Matters conducted as part of its evaluation. Mrs. Bernstein took these interviews to heart, even as she wished that there were better, less threatening ways for her to offer suggestions, critiques, and encouragement.

"At one point," she acknowledges, "Arthur said to me, 'If you want to run the school, then you'd better pack your bags and move to San Francisco. Because you can't do it from here, and you can't do it part-time.' And he was right. But I wasn't going to move to San Francisco. And I wasn't going to do it full-time. Because I'd only micromanage it to death." The gradual diminution of Keren Keshet's financial support to the school in more recent years has also put greater distance between the funders and the school's leadership, leaving more space for creative conversations that do not carry the murky suggestion of meddling. It helped that the foundation's confidence in Rabbi Ruben ran high, so that it was easier for Mrs. Bernstein and Mr. Fried to take a more arms-length approach to their relationship with the school, trusting in his expertise and sound judgment.

In truth, the tensions between educators and funders at the Jewish Community High School were hardly unique in the world of philanthropy. Funders who create new institutions and facilities often feel, as Mr. Fried put it in another context, not like funders but like owners. Here was a school that literally would not have existed, except as a brief experiment, but for the scores of millions of dollars that Keren Keshet poured into it. It would have been a rare funder indeed who, in these circumstances, would not have felt a "pride of ownership" and tried to ensure that huge dreams and huge investment produced huge results. In fact, many of those who expressed frustration at Keren Keshet's involvement in decision-making at the school nonetheless acknowledged that, as one board member put it, "the financial resources that the foundation has been providing have allowed us to really do things that we could not have done organically." In the world of large-scale grantmaking, big gifts produce not only gratitude but, almost inevitably, some amount of anxiety.

At the time this is written, the Jewish Community High School of the Bay is not the institution Mrs. Bernstein dreamed it would be. That, too, is an experience with which many big donors can sympathize: Money can buy many fine things, but it can rarely incarnate a dream. Instead, as she and Mr. Fried readily agree, it is an outstanding school and, more specific to their dreams, an outstanding *Jewish* school. Its students get a rich Jewish education accompanied by a distinguished curriculum of secular subjects from science and math to the arts and humanities. Its graduates become adults who are more likely than many of their peers to surround themselves with Jewish friends, date or marry Jewish partners, visit and care about Israel, and derive at least a portion of their identity from their Jewish heritage.

"The school worked out fine," Mr. Fried concluded in an interview in 2021. "It's 20 years later. It's still there. It's still operating. This term, it has the most students it's ever had. Many of its graduates have gone on to live in Israel and serve in the [Israel Defense Forces]. They've gone to fine universities. They enrich the Jewish world. And the school has a distinguished principal, a good man, a good educator, runs a wonderful school. He made it a solid educational institution."

"Is that everything it could be?" Mrs. Bernstein added. "Maybe so, maybe not. But the fact that hundreds of kids were in a Jewish high school, and got a good Jewish education there besides all the other subjects, is a real leg up—for them, for the Jewish community. It's a real accomplishment."

CHAPTER III

'PORTALS OF DISCOVERY'

The Creation of Nextbook and Tablet

Keren Keshet's embrace of the Jewish Community Library of San Francisco was only one manifestation of its trustees' interest in books and libraries, and far from the largest one. Through the AVI CHAI Foundation, they supported libraries in Jewish day schools, sponsored scholarly commentaries on classic texts, and donated starter sets of essential Jewish books to day school students. Through the Tikvah Fund, they underwrote writing by influential Jewish authors and published *The Jewish Review of Books*. And more than either of those two charities, under the stewardship of Mrs. Bernstein and Mr. Fried Keren Keshet became a living encyclopedia of Jewish literary philanthropy, supporting libraries and book-related programs in schools, community centers, cultural venues, public festivals—almost any place where Jewish life might draw nourishment from Jewish writing. Of all these efforts, the largest by far was the long-running philanthropic adventure that came to be known as *Tablet*.

The idea was born in 1999, during an afternoon visit to San Francisco's main public library, whose \$126 million renovation and expansion was then just three years old.[27] Strolling through the various reading rooms and dedicated centers—one for African American literature and references, one for books in Chinese or about Chinese culture, one dedicated to the Filipino-American experience, and several others besides—Mr. Fried and Mrs. Bernstein noticed a peculiar omission. Despite a wall of names recognizing donors to the library—a list that featured a constellation of prominent Jewish philanthropists from across the Bay Area—the building had no Jewish Center or any single place where a patron could search for Jewish topics, authors, or texts.

The reason was innocent, though still disappointing. The idea of creating these dedicated rooms had arisen late in the library's fundraising campaign, after most of the major Bay Area donors, including the Jewish ones, had already subscribed. The library's development team had come up with the idea as a way of appealing to special-interest donors who would not otherwise make a general gift to the library for its own sake. A prime example was the Michigan-based Kresge Foundation, which had a programmatic interest in services for immigrants but not in libraries *per se*. Kresge made a sizable grant to create an International Center that now houses the Chinese and Filipino collections along with extensive resources for other immigrant groups.

Whatever the reason, the lack of Jewish collections in libraries struck Mrs. Bernstein and Mr. Fried as a gap that cried out to be filled—not only, or even necessarily, in San Francisco, but everywhere. And it seemed to be a project perfectly suited to philanthropy. Neither governments nor businesses would likely single out one ethnic group for their largesse, and as the San Francisco reading rooms showed, libraries would do so only if donors showed an interest and provided the wherewithal. This was something Keren Keshet could do, and something close to the bull's-eye of its mission. For a Jewish seeker not yet ready to embrace a synagogue or commit to religious education, or even to visit a Jewish community center, what better place to start a journey of Jewish exploration—to examine the "single white light refracted through a moisture-laden sky"—than in a welcoming public place where the whole rainbow was on display, without conditions or restrictions, waiting to be explored?

To chart a path forward, the foundation's trustees first turned to a longtime friend, an observant Jew, and a nationally known expert in philanthropy, Joel L. Fleishman of Duke University. He, in turn, recommended bringing on a consultant who could devote substantial time to surveying the field, gathering opinions from librarians and other knowledgeable sources, and formulating a set of options. And he had just the person in mind: Julie Sandorf, a skilled nonprofit *macher* who had been a protégé of the legendary (and Jewish) Ford Foundation executive Mitchell Sviridoff.

It was hardly an obvious choice. Ms. Sandorf had made her reputation first in the field of urban development, beginning in the South Bronx and then extending more widely. Her most recent achievement had been the creation of a national nonprofit to combat homelessness, called the Corporation for Supportive Housing. In that capacity she had become a national leader in reforming U.S. homeless policy. She had consulted for some of America's best-known foundations on employment and youth programs. But, as she succinctly put it, "there was not a single thing on my résumé that says 'Jewish.'"

Still, in Professor Fleishman's eyes, Ms. Sandorf neatly fit the bill in two crucial respects. First, she was a social entrepreneur. She had

built durable programs and institutions from the ground up, and she
had an uncanny eye for talent. Her efforts in community development
and homelessness had attracted gifted young people who rose to become leaders in their own right, ultimately taking over the reins from
Ms. Sandorf as she moved on to other ventures.

Second, although there was no space for such a thing on a résumé,
Ms. Sandorf was very close to the kind of person that Keren Keshet
hoped to reach. She is Jewish, but she was not religious, not at that
point affiliated with any Jewish causes or institutions, and only glanc-
ingly acquainted with Jewish letters and culture. Nonetheless, she had
very recently set out on her own journey of understanding her Jewish
heritage, and that journey had started primarily with books.

After one meeting, Mr. Fried and Mrs. Bernstein liked what they
saw and asked Ms. Sandorf to scope out the practical possibilities for
creating what they called "Jewish libraries." Was this a field where the
foundation could exert influence? Would libraries be open to the idea
of creating and staffing Judaic reading rooms? Would libraries be
fertile ground for assembling worthy collections, effective programs,
and what Mr. Fried (perhaps borrowing from James Joyce) called
"portals of discovery"? If the prospects seemed promising, where and
how should they get started?

As Ms. Sandorf set out on her reconnaissance, Mr. Fried penned
a memo to the files. If the idea could be shown to be feasible, he wrote,
Keren Keshet "would be prepared to fund, over an extended period,
let us begin with possibly ten years, the acquisitions budget, personnel
costs, and activities program" of the Jewish culture and literature
departments in major Jewish population centers. "Our principal goal
is to find locales which could benefit from this kind of 'secular' Jewish
outreach."

Ms. Sandorf filed her first report early in 2000, confidently dispatching three concerns that might have seemed, on first glance, to threaten the feasibility of the project. First, creating Jewish centers in public libraries would pose no legal obstacle to the libraries' status as either government agencies or publicly supported nonprofits. American courts had long recognized "Jewish" as an ethnic identity independent of religious belief, so explicitly Jewish programs and services would be no less legitimate in public libraries than Chinese or African-American ones. (That doesn't mean the issue wouldn't arise, of course. The head of one large urban library system refused to even consider the idea, on the grounds that it would be "perceived as religious.")

Second, although technology seemed destined to disrupt the traditional model of public libraries as repositories and lenders of physical books, Ms. Sandorf's sources remained confident that brick-and-mortar libraries would remain vital, even as they scrambled to accommodate e-books and other digital content. In fact, in the Internet age, librarians may prove to be more important than ever, helping patrons to navigate the boundless and chaotic world of online information.

Third, just as Mrs. Bernstein and Mr. Fried surmised, specialized collections are common in the library world, so the idea of creating new ones would, in most cases, require no special pleading—provided, of course, the money was sufficient. But a specialized *Jewish* collection would indeed be breaking new ground. After months of research, Ms. Sandorf had been able to find only one Jewish department in any major American library system, and that one was the exception that proved the rule. "The New York Public Library's Dorot Jewish Division at the main branch," she wrote, is "a very scholarly place for serious theologians and researchers. It's not a place a casual reader would walk into." So here was a concept that, just as the foundation trustees had imagined, would introduce something altogether new into the American cultural landscape. And it would fill a void that, in their view, had long been a disservice to both Jewish and American letters.

The only flashing yellow light in Ms. Sandorf's first report was a warning about one hypothetical approach to organizing the project—a warning that would eventually have wider implications. Mr. Fried and Mrs. Bernstein had imagined that Keren Keshet's role would include purchasing books for libraries, helping them create suitable browsing and reading spaces, and paying for a dedicated Jewish librarian. This person would help patrons find things that interested them and would generally conduct the "secular outreach" that Mr. Fried's memo had described. But Ms. Sandorf was warned that libraries would not welcome or even accept such special-purpose employees, especially ones chosen by outsiders. "Libraries do not have much flexibility when it comes to specialized staffing," she wrote, because of Civil Service requirements and established hierarchies of credentials and seniority. "It may be difficult, if not impossible, to designate and fund a new staff position within the regular staffing patterns of the library."

Still, assuming this one obstacle could be averted, the report presented a strong argument for moving forward. Next, Ms. Sandorf suggested, the foundation should marshal some expertise in constructing a Jewish library program. "My report said: Yes, it's possible," she recounted some years later. "But we need somebody working with us who *really knows* Jewish culture and literature—because I don't."

The person she found was Jonathan Rosen, who at that point was stepping down as cultural editor of *The Forward*, a venerable Jewish weekly that was then in the throes of a boardroom coup. A journalist and novelist, well acquainted with New York's Jewish literary and intellectual circles, Mr. Rosen was most recently the author of a soon-to-be-published book on Jewish heritage in the information age (*The Talmud and the Internet: A Journey Between Worlds*, Farrar, Straus and Giroux, September 2000). Ms. Sandorf asked him to prepare a concept paper, suggesting ways the foundation could define and begin implementing a Jewish library program.

Mr. Rosen's paper started with a reflection on the lack of specifically Jewish collections in American libraries as both a shortcoming and a triumph for Jewish Americans. On one hand, he pointed out, Jewish writing is so thoroughly woven into American letters that a collection that fully represented Judaism's contribution would be impractically large. On the other hand, cultural self-discovery is a hallmark of late 20th century American society, and Jews have no less need of it, or desire for it, than other ethnic minorities. The challenge for Keren Keshet, he concluded, is to create "a new Jewish library for a new age."

In what would become a significant variation on Mr. Fried's and Mrs. Bernstein's original idea for "Jewish libraries"—plural—Mr. Rosen's paper dwelt extensively on the idea of "what constitutes a modern Jewish library," singular. Much of the paper is a meditation on what a defensible syllabus of key Jewish writing would contain, a list that might then become the core collection that Keren Keshet would donate to participating libraries as the cornerstone of the project. Mr. Rosen had in mind something akin to the Harvard Library of Classics—a close-to-canonical bookshelf of what a liberally educated person should read.

Keren Keshet circulated Mr. Rosen's paper to 15 Jewish scholars, educators, and writers, and then invited them to gather for a day and a half of discussion in the National Hall in Westport, Connecticut, on September 24, 2000. A few days later, in a written summary of the proceedings, Ms. Sandorf reported broad support for the idea of establishing Jewish collections and dedicated librarians in public libraries, but ambivalence about anointing a "Jewish canon" in the tradition of the Harvard Classics. Some participants doubted that there would be much agreement on what constituted either an essential Jewish corpus or useful introductory reading. Even lifelong scholars, some argued, would have a hard time reaching a consensus, and people who are still tentatively approaching Judaism might have needs or interests that scholars wouldn't foresee.

Instead, the group focused most of its attention on libraries and librarians, much as Mrs. Bernstein and Mr. Fried had originally done. "The single most important element in achieving our goals," Ms. Sandorf wrote in her notes from the meeting, "is developing a cadre of 'shepherds' . . . who can act as educators, guides, and intellectual entrepreneurs." Despite her earlier warning on the difficulty of getting libraries to put such "shepherds" on their own payrolls, it was clear to Ms. Sandorf that this idea of a human face for the project in each participating community carried a certain magic for the people in Westport. Civil service and other impediments notwithstanding, placing the right "entrepreneurs" in libraries, and in contact with people seeking inroads into Judaism, would need to be close to the center of the effort.

The primary challenge would not be selecting and shipping books, but what Mr. Fried had called "outreach." In this respect, she wrote, the core purpose of the project should be creating "a sense of community" for Jews with no other source of affiliation with their heritage or sense of fellowship in Jewish culture. Compared with that, settling on a "required reading" list of classic titles would be less important. Assembling a rich, diverse, representative list of good Jewish books to recommend to libraries, and adjusting that list with advice from the "shepherds," would probably be sufficient. The goal was not necessarily that people should read the *right* books on Judaism, but that they should read *more* Jewish books, and want more still.

Guided by the advice and enthusiasm of the Westport participants, Ms. Sandorf and Mr. Rosen set out to put flesh on the concept and envision a structure and budget. Their idea centered on the "shepherds," whom they tentatively named Keren Keshet Library Fellows: an "elite corps of 'intellectual entrepreneurs' who will serve as educators, marketers, and intermediaries for [Jewish culture and literature] in public libraries." They would not be library employees, but they would be partners and resources for libraries, and spend significant time on their premises. Standing behind them would be a national program that would recruit, fund, supply, and manage the fellows, besides distributing books.

The national program would be a "signature program" of Keren Keshet, a separately incorporated "operating arm," governed by an independent board. Fellows would then be employees of the national nonprofit organization but assigned to libraries, working on library premises, with a local advisory committee to guide their programming. This arrangement would presumably make the fellows more palatable to library managers, who would not have to put the fellows on their payroll, but could use the "intellectual entrepreneurs" as a source of quality programming.

———

Ms. Sandorf and Mr. Rosen spelled out this structure in a revised concept paper for the Keshet trustees in 2001. But in addition to the distribution of books and the deployment of fellows, they suggested a possible third component: "establishing a companion-publishing venture that would create the definition of a modern Jewish library . . . a prototypical, uniform collection of texts that Americans could not only encounter in public libraries, but could visit on the Web and could ultimately obtain for their own homes."

The idea had arisen partly from a conversation the pair had had with Michael Terry, then the chief librarian of the New York Public Library's Jewish Division. Mr. Terry had not been especially enthusiastic about the prospect of "Jewish libraries" and fellows and public programs—he considered it all a bit amorphous and was skeptical that a wide audience would flock to it. But "if you were *making something*," Mr. Rosen remembers him saying, "people would like that. They want things that are new."

It was a surprising remark from a curator of old, sometimes ancient, volumes. But it sounded right to Mr. Rosen. "The thought stuck with me," he said later. "I kept thinking about it." But the more he worked through the practical implications of creating a new, popular treatment of classic Jewish texts, the more obstacles he hit.

For starters, the collection would have to include texts originally written in Hebrew, Aramaic, Arabic, Judeo-Arabic, or Yiddish, whose English translations, if they exist at all, tend to be scholarly and not meant for general, secular audiences. Commissioning new translations of all this material would be expensive, and authors with the right combination of skills to do the job well—the expertise to interpret the texts, plus the literary flair to make them sing to a modern audience—would be vanishingly few. The Westport group had been skeptical of creating a Jewish "Harvard Classics" partly for these reasons.

And on reflection, Mr. Rosen had to agree with them. The foundational written works of Judaism, he realized, are "not books you *read*, they're books you *study*." Many of the critical texts are inherently dense and would be hard for inexpert readers to follow, no matter how good the translation. Even the most knowledgeable readers tend to devote years of study and inquiry to discerning the meaning of these books. Far from being a collection that would entice people into deeper and deeper exploration, the books might just as likely intimidate the neophyte into abandoning all interest in Jewish reading. "So why on earth would we do this?" he asked. "Just so people could have them on their shelves?"

At that point, Michael Terry's original comment replayed in Mr. Rosen's mind with new meaning. He thought: What if "*making* something, something original, meant there was something *we could create*" that might actually rescue the classic texts from obscurity and lower the barrier for modern Jews who would benefit from encountering them? "Maybe we ought to create *original* books that are encounters between modern writers and classical authors, between the Jewish present and Jewish heritage."

Fortunately, this idea of an encounter between modern thinkers and great figures of the past had a recent precedent—in fact, a commercially successful one—in American publishing. Barely five years earlier, investment banker Kenneth Lipper, a friend of Mr. Fried, had launched a similar project in partnership with publisher Viking/Penguin, in which modern writers (but not necessarily biographers) wrote brief lives of historical figures, infusing the story with the authors' own, modern perspective. After a conversation with Mr. Lipper, Mem Bernstein felt a flash of inspiration. "We could do this," she remembers thinking. "We could have a series like this one, but focused on Jewish lives." It wouldn't be long before she discovered that her idea nicely dovetailed with the approach Mr. Rosen was starting to envision.

Many of the ten "Penguin Lives" then in Mr. Lipper's series involved author/subject pairings like the encounters Mr. Rosen had in mind—writers who shared ethnic or spiritual affinities with their subjects, and for whom writing the biography was partly an act of personal homage or pilgrimage. Lipper's titles included Catholics Mary Gordon and Garry Wills writing on Saints Joan of Arc and Augustine of Hippo, respectively. Irish expatriate novelist Edna O'Brien wrote the life of her wandering Hibernian forebear James Joyce. Edmund White, dean of American gay literati, produced a portrait of Marcel Proust struggling with his sexual identity. In these cases, as in the series Mr. Rosen imagined producing, he concluded that "the idea of an *encounter* is more than just one writer commenting on another. It's two parts of a culture coming to a point of meeting." In a series of such encounters, to borrow Mr. Fried's terms, perhaps the refracted lights of the Jewish rainbow could be drawn closer to the "original bright white light" of essential Judaism.

Mr. Fried, Mrs. Bernstein, and Ms. Sandorf found this argument persuasive, and in early January 2001, on the recommendation of the literary agent Andrew Wylie, Mr. Rosen began what eventually became three months of negotiations with Schocken Books and its parent company, Alfred A. Knopf, about the publication of a "Jewish Encounters" series. By midyear, names of authors and potential subjects were being passed back and forth between Mr. Rosen, who was designated the series editor, and Dan Frank, representing Schocken and Knopf.

The initial pairings of modern authors with historical figures— Robert Pinsky on King David, Stephen Dubner on Moses, Rebecca Goldstein on Spinoza, Sherwin Nuland on Maimonides—soon attracted interest from other authors whose eye was drawn to more recent or less monumental Jewish lives. These newer projects included

Esther Schor on poet Emma Lazarus, Doug Century on boxer and World War II hero Barney Ross, Seth Lipsky on Abraham Cahan, first editor of *The Forward*. Eventually—and after some soul-searching among people involved with the project—the series outgrew its initial focus on biography, to include encounters with Jewish-historical *themes*, not just people. Contracts for later books included illustrator Ben Katchor on the peculiar institution of the Jewish dairy restaurant, playwright David Mamet on anti-Semitism, and Mexican-Jewish-American sociolinguist Ilan Stavans on the resurgence of Hebrew as a living language.

With a unifying graphic identity created by designer and publisher William Drenttel, the book series came together quickly and distinctively. The first two volumes, on David and Maimonides, were in bookstores in the autumn of 2005.

———

While the idea for the book series was still taking shape, Julie Sandorf was focusing primarily on the libraries and programs, assembling lists of possible fellows, scoping out places to assign them, and clarifying what, exactly, their work would consist of. She had originally joined the project solely as a consultant, to draw up a concept and operating plan and to help recruit top staff, including not only the library fellows but also a permanent director. However, after more than a year of searching, tapping her own networks as well as those of Mrs. Bernstein, Mr. Fried, and Mr. Rosen, no strong candidate had emerged. The Keren Keshet trustees had become convinced that the best person for the job by far was Ms. Sandorf herself, but that was not going to be an easy case to make to her.

Her earlier experience creating a new nonprofit had been spiritually and professionally fulfilling, but physically and mentally exhausting. She had grown weary of constant fundraising, frustrated with administrative minutiae, and wary of the mercurial interests of many foundations, whose support, in her experience, tended to move in inverse, rather than direct, proportion to success. She had made all this clear to Mr. Fried and Mrs. Bernstein, and gently but firmly declined their initial offer. But their response both amazed her and won her over.

Unbidden, they made four commitments that, one by one, dispelled all her reasons for resisting. First, they offered a roughly ten-year commitment that would continue or increase, not diminish, if the project succeeded. ("To anyone not familiar with foundations," Ms. Sandorf said some years later, "that may sound obvious. But in my experience, it was really extraordinary.") Second, they offered to keep the project for a time as a resident activity of Keren Keshet, so that she could concentrate more on program development than on administration. (The project eventually incorporated as an independent nonprofit in early 2004.) Third, they recognized that she had other consulting commitments and could not immediately begin working full-time. Assuming she could assemble a staff to cover all the full-time needs of the organization, the foundation would be content with a three-day-a-week leader for a while. And finally, Keren Keshet would cover the full cost of the project for the time being, so that no other fundraising would be required for basic operations. Ms. Sandorf agreed, and in March 2002 she officially took over the project.

Over the course of several months of travel and research, she had tentatively settled on three metropolitan library systems in which to get started: Greater Chicago, Seattle, and Washington, D.C. With Mr. Fried's and Mrs. Bernstein's approval of this list, she then went about recruiting five Fellows for the three programs—two each for Chicago and Washington, to work separately with urban and suburban library systems, and one in Seattle serving the whole metropolitan area.

Hewing to the original program concept, she chose people mainly for their knowledge of Jewish literature and the literary scene in each city, not necessarily for any expertise in the business of managing and marketing public programs. Yet it quickly became clear that, without high-quality programs and activities to whet people's literary appetites, the number of library patrons seeking out Jewish resources on their own would be minuscule. For real *outreach*, the fellows would have to be partly impresarios. So, within weeks of starting on the job, they found themselves grappling with the unfamiliar challenges of booking authors and venues for public readings and lectures, and reaching out to audiences, as a way of spotlighting and promoting Jewish literature. Lacking any in-house expertise in these areas, Ms. Sandorf sought a senior manager with credentials in literary programming to oversee and guide the local programs.

In her travels, she had come upon Matthew Brogan, director of Seattle Arts and Lectures, a widely respected presenting organization for literary programming, who had also impressed Mrs. Bernstein with his combination of literary and management savvy. Luring Mr. Brogan to the East Coast from a coveted and highly rewarding position in Seattle was not an immediately promising prospect. But from Mrs. Bernstein's living room in Jerusalem, she and Mr. Fried phoned him with a direct appeal: Here, they suggested, is an opportunity to create something new, national, and groundbreaking—backed by hands-on funders who would support him in every way, both material and practical. It would be exceedingly rare in the world of nonprofit arts organizations to find funders as personally devoted to his success as they would be. He took the position in early 2003 and started a few months later.

To assemble an initial set of books for the participating libraries to offer, and for speakers to spotlight in in-person events, Ms. Sandorf took counsel from Columbia University Professor Jeremy Dauber, an expert in Hebrew and Yiddish literature who was already an adviser to Keren Keshet and to the AVI CHAI Foundation. (He later wrote a biography of Sholem Aleichem for the Jewish Encounters series.) Although compiling the reading list was supposed to have been Professor Dauber's main task, the fellows and other staff quickly took to asking his advice more broadly. He became what Ms. Sandorf started calling the "shepherds' shepherd"—the resident scholar and critic who could advise other staff members on the quality and integrity of the project's Jewish literary content. He started a kind of in-house professional development program to help staff deepen their understanding of classic Jewish texts and their effect on later thought and writing, including an in-depth weekly seminar on the Bible.

With Mr. Brogan coordinating, and using Mr. Drenttel's design scheme, the fellows quickly produced a set of promotional materials, including posters and flyers to be displayed and distributed in libraries and book stores, and a syllabus of recommended books drawn from Professor Dauber's reading list. They sketched out a program of readings, lectures, book groups, children's activities, and other events based on the recommended books, which they hoped to persuade libraries to host. But bringing these plans to life meant navigating the libraries' distinctive bureaucracies, with their complex systems for approval and allocation of space and equipment. The result was often not the kind of hand-in-hand partnership that Keren Keshet had hoped for, and getting the events off the ground turned out to be a slow and sometimes arduous process.

For instance, the Seattle Public Library, despite early signs of enthusiasm, soon grew distant when the time came for actual activity, and cooperation from its staff dwindled almost to zero. The Chicago suburban libraries, many of which were highly supportive, are nonetheless all divided into separate, independent systems, and coordination of events among the suburban libraries with large Jewish populations proved fiendishly difficult. Even in generally supportive and well-coordinated environments like the Seattle suburbs, the Chicago city libraries, and Washington, D.C., the fellows found that branch librarians rarely had much time to spend with them and could provide only minimal help in scheduling, arranging logistics, distributing public information, or integrating the new project into regular library operations. Programs and displays did begin to materialize, starting in the fall of 2003, but their progress was slower than originally planned.

Neither did bookstores turn out to be especially fruitful partners in the early years. Ms. Sandorf had worked out an agreement, in exchange for a fee, by which the American Booksellers' Association would periodically distribute to its member stores a stack of reading lists, sleekly designed in bright colors, aimed at whetting customers' appetites for important Jewish titles. But in subsequent visits to bookstores and interviews with shop owners, she discovered that the association's mailings were often discarded without ever being opened. Even when someone opened them, the Keren Keshet reading lists were relegated, at best, to tables full of other flyers and brochures where hardly anyone would notice them. The most promising thing the booksellers told Ms. Sandorf was that they would be more interested in promotional materials related to new publications—a promising thought for Mr. Rosen's forthcoming series, but otherwise not much help at the moment.

The fellows found their greatest success with what became known as the Writers Series, consisting of public lectures and readings by prominent Jewish authors. These often occurred in library auditoriums and community rooms, thus making them officially part of the public libraries' programming, though many ended up taking place at universities or Jewish Community Centers that could accommodate crowds better than most libraries. In any case, they were special events, not routine activities integrated into the branch libraries' daily or weekly schedule. Fellows had to do most of the heavy lifting in booking the venues, arranging the logistics, and promoting and managing the events. Other, lower-profile activities like book clubs were similarly up to the fellows to plan, set up, and execute, without much help from library staff.

Crowds for the Writers Series were usually sizable enough to give it cachet and a feeling of cultural importance. But on closer inspection, they didn't seem to be breaking much ground in attracting a new, curious clientele seeking unknown "portals of discovery." In their frequent visits to these events, Mr. Fried and Mrs. Bernstein found that many of the attendees were already regular fans of book readings, lectures, and book clubs. A substantial proportion already attended other Jewish events and institutions. Average ages skewed high, even for up-and-coming authors whose writing should have appealed to younger audiences as well.

As the trustees pressed for a less established, less traditionally literary audience, the fellows increasingly found themselves searching beyond the upholstered silence of libraries and lecture halls. Their next effort was to organize less formal events in what they called the Readings and Performances Series in pubs, theaters, music halls, and other trendy cultural settings where younger people congregate. By early 2005, Chicago's Beat Kitchen and Abbey Pub, and Seattle's Rendezvous Pub and Big Picture Theater were at least as likely to be the settings for foundation-sponsored events as the libraries' formal auditoriums and conference rooms. In the Readings and Performances series, prominent Jewish cultural figures like broadcaster Susan Stamberg or novelists Jeffery Eugenides, Gary Shteyngart, and Esther Freud held forth on stages whose previous occupant, or the next one, would likely have been a blues singer or a punk band.

There was a trade-off here, of course, and it was the subject of frequent debate back in the project's headquarters: In exchange for presenting cutting-edge Jewish literature to fresh audiences, were the programs drifting too far from Keren Keshet's original idea of opening minds to serious personal exploration and reflection? Given the high quality of the speakers and readers, the programs could hardly be accused of dumbing down their message, strictly speaking. But were they packaging and selling it so aggressively that the end result was mere entertainment—a cursory glance at something Jewish, followed by a rock concert?

Anxiety about taking the edginess too far was never far from the fellows' minds, although Mrs. Bernstein and Mr. Fried were careful to give them wide latitude for experimentation and learning. So even as their beer-hall programming was becoming more and more popular, most of their work still concentrated on eminent Jewish artists and scholars discussing serious issues in formal settings. The programs continued, constantly striking and adjusting the balance, for another three years—until the financial crash of 2008 caused the Keren Keshet trustees to take another look.

———

During the early months of 2000 and 2001 when the project was taking shape, Mr. Fried, Mrs. Bernstein, and Ms. Sandorf had been referring to it by a handful of informal names, which tended to shift over time. The trustees started off informally calling it "Jewish Libraries," then "Jewish Libraries and Books." Ms. Sandorf started off with "the Library and Lives Project," and later "Encountering Great Jewish Lives and Literature." But all of these were just descriptive phrases. None had the ring of a brand, a permanent name for a new organization that sought to make an impression on a wide public. In the early months of scrambling to assemble a staff; build relationships with libraries, authors, and a publisher; and plan initial public activities, no one yet felt any urgency about coming up with a corporate name.

But then, in 2002, as Mr. Drenttel was drawing up designs for publications, promotional materials and stationery—all of which still had placeholders where the organization's name would go—he raised an offhand question that prompted a big decision. "What are you going to do," he asked, "about your website?"

Ms. Sandorf admits having given the question almost no thought at all. "Site?" she asked herself. "I hadn't even thought about having a site. I guess I kind of assumed we'd have one, but I had no idea what it would be for, or even when we would start dealing with it." Many outlines and descriptions of the project, dating to Mr. Rosen's earliest concept paper, had referred to a role for the Internet, but the specifics were yet to be discussed. Mr. Drenttel's question prompted the sudden realization that some kind of web presence would be necessary right away, and it would probably become more and more necessary as a programming tool before long. But a website has to start with a domain name—not a placeholder, but an actual name.

In his thoughts about a website, Mr. Drenttel was envisioning something more than just a useful place to post program information. As it happens, he had been a board member of a company that, at the time, owned the influential website *Arts & Letters Daily*, which linked readers to current intellectual and cultural offerings throughout the

World Wide Web. Amid all the discussion about creating a "portal" or "gateway" to Jewish culture—terms that had consistently been used in their general, pre-Internet sense, as metaphors for points of access—Mr. Drenttel almost automatically thought of the newer and more specific meaning of "portal": a website that serves as a starting point to discover other destinations on the Web.

"I'm sitting there hearing about scholars and libraries," he said, "about portals to Jewish literature, and it just seemed to me like the *Arts & Letters Daily* model. A kind of 'Jewish Culture and Literature Daily,' though obviously not by that name." Intrigued, Ms. Sandorf went to her computer, opened aldaily.com, and immediately fell in love with the concept. She asked Mr. Drenttel to design a simple prototype, and within a couple of weeks it was ready for Mrs. Bernstein and Mr. Fried.

Their reaction surprised and delighted him. "I showed them the prototype at that first meeting," Mr. Drenttel recalled, "and they said in effect, 'Go build it.' This meant [spending] new money—for the site, for equipment, for an editor. It was completely unbudgeted. But they just went for it."

The decision was quick but careful. Mr. Fried explained later that the trustees were able to give the project a green light in part because it was "high potential return with relatively low risk." The site as presented was just one page and simple in concept. It could be built and launched with a comparatively small investment, then expanded only if its quality and readership seemed to justify it. In the meantime, the additional personnel costs, though hardly negligible, would not be burdensome. *Arts & Letters Daily* was produced, for the most part, by a staff of two; the simpler design of this project could be maintained by a single part-time staffer. The audience, as Mr. Fried saw it, was "practically universal, but the initial investment could be quite small."

The trustees' approval meant the need for a brand name, and thus a domain name, was now immediate. Worryingly, no one had yet come up with anything remotely distinctive or catchy enough to qualify. Even the most basic issues had yet to be resolved: Should "Jewish" be in the name? Or would that be off-putting to unaffiliated Jews who weren't ready to make a commitment to an avowedly Jewish enterprise? Should the name refer to books specifically, or culture more generally? Was it even possible for one name to encompass what were now three separate lines of work: library programs, book publishing, and a website?

Some weeks before the question of a website arose, Ms. Sandorf and Mr. Rosen had been talking about the library project with Nessa Rapoport, a writer and editor who was, at the time, director of publications for the Mandel Foundation. Imagining the kind of seeker Keren Keshet hoped to attract, Ms. Rapoport recalled a blurb that Saul Bellow had written for Primo Levi's story collection *The Periodic Table*: "We are always looking for the book it is necessary to read next." The quotation particularly appealed to Mr. Rosen, who thought of using it as a unifying epigraph on all the books in his Jewish Encounters series.

A month or so later, when the discussion of a project name began to percolate, Mr. Rosen thought again about the Bellow quote, with its evocation of cultural curiosity, of seeking, and of the necessity of the search. Weren't those, in essence, the motivating ideas behind this whole project? The search for the *next book*, whether in a library, in a bookstore, in a publisher's catalogue, or on the web, seemed like the heart of what Keren Keshet had envisioned when it launched the effort. Perhaps, then, the *next book* should be in the name. Why not call it Nextbook?*

---

* The name sounds slightly less exotic today than it did at the time. Two years after the creation of Nextbook, a Harvard sophomore named Mark Zuckerberg launched what he initially called The Facebook, a very different kind of website but with a similar compound name.

Ms. Sandorf and Mr. Drenttel both liked it, and in the absence of any comparably snappy alternatives, "Nextbook" shot to the top of the list of possibilities. The other candidates generally had fewer strengths and more weaknesses. "Eternal Library," a leading contender early in the search, struck some people as sepulchral. "Pomegranate" and "Olive Branch" both had Jewish cultural and religious connotations, but were generally considered too subtle or off-topic (Recipes? Horticulture? Antiwar efforts?). "The Chosen Book" struck a chord with some, but others feared that "chosen" might carry subtly exclusive connotations. Other candidates similarly seemed either too explicit or too vague; some were drab, others dangerously exotic. The longer the search went on, the better "Nextbook" sounded.

It had its disadvantages, of course. It was, admittedly, less than specific. Still, as a later employee in the project pointed out, "It does provoke curiosity, which is the main thing you want it to do." The lack of anything Jewish in the name struck some as a peculiar omission, but most people saw it, on balance, as an asset: Mr. Fried had wanted "no barriers to entry," and "Nextbook's" lack of visible ethnicity made it a genuinely no-barrier proposition.

Best of all, there was something dynamic, intriguing, even slightly provocative about the "next" in the title. It held out the tantalizing promise, as Michael Terry of the New York Public Library had put it, of "things that are new." Mr. Drenttel also noted one aspect of the idea that was likely to appeal to the funders: It was a new coinage, unassociated with any other endeavor, and thus inexpensive to register as a domain name. Despite some hesitancy over the ambiguity of the proposed name, Mr. Fried and Mrs. Bernstein saw its advantages, too. In the end, with no serious objections that would make them overrule their creative team, they approved the choice, and Nextbook was born.

Now, the new domain needed a webmaster, and Mr. Rosen had a candidate in mind. Blake Eskin, a former colleague at *The Forward* and a recently published author, was working as webmaster at the Council on Foreign Relations. It was a prestige job, but the buttoned-down world of diplomacy wasn't really Mr. Eskin's style. When Ms. Sandorf interviewed him over lunch in late 2002, she found him by far the strongest of a handful of candidates she'd been considering. For his part, Mr. Eskin liked the challenge of starting something new and the opportunity to return to the realm of creativity and culture, where he felt most at home. He started in November and had a website ready to launch the following May.

In the interim, Mr. Eskin spent several weeks testing various combinations of content and style, first by sending e-mails to a circle of test readers, then by producing an actual web page that only the test group could access. Roughly following the model of *Arts & Letters Daily*, the pilot site featured a deliberately broad mix of topics—a cocktail of religion, the arts, politics, scholarship, and popular culture—in proportions calculated to be neither too highbrow nor too low. Each entry had to be brief and be inviting enough to pique interest—clever but not glib, thoughtful but not stuffy, in language equally appealing to younger and older readers. When the pilot ended and Nextbook.org went live, it had developed a look and feel quite different from Arts & Letters Daily, but it was still strictly an index to other articles on the web, with no original articles, only Mr. Eskin's brief teasers to help a reader decide where to go and what to read next.

That changed after about a year, when Mr. Eskin and a newly hired associate editor began writing and commissioning Nextbook-only content: interviews, features, reflections on trends. This experiment with original material reflected a gradual but ultimately significant departure from the site's initial concept. First the descriptions of linked material grew longer, and now the staff's own observations and commentary was starting to move closer to center stage. Before long, Nextbook.org had become not just a roadmap to the rest of the Jewish web, but a destination in its own right, with articles that could be found nowhere else. It was becoming an online magazine of Jewish culture.

Reader reaction was positive, and traffic was ticking steadily upward, though measurement of such things was still primitive by the standards of later decades. Regardless, this was new terrain, not yet explicitly embraced by Keren Keshet. And it packed some real risks. "We would be putting ourselves forward," Ms. Sandorf said soon after the new material started to appear, "perceived as speaking on behalf of the foundation, about things that might—not intentionally, maybe, but might—be perceived as taking sides on controversial issues. Did we really want to be doing that? Especially now, before we're really known for anything else?"

More to the point, did the Keshet trustees want them to be doing that? The growth of blogging and online journalism in the prior decade had been driven largely by political writing. Pioneering bloggers like Andrew Sullivan, Josh Marshall, and Mickey Kaus were drawing bigger and bigger audiences largely through provocative coverage and commentary on current political controversies. That sort of thing was the most proven way to attract eyeballs and clicks, but it was not what Nextbook had been created to do.

As the website evolved more and more toward becoming an online magazine, with its own features, style, and distinctive mix of topics, one of the few constraints Ms. Sandorf felt was what she took to be an injunction from Mrs. Bernstein and Mr. Fried not to let the site stray from Keren Keshet's original purpose: to draw Jews toward a greater awareness of, and curiosity about, their cultural and religious heritage. If the website became a magazine, that was fine with the trustees—so long as it was a Jewish cultural magazine that supported the rest of the organization's mission.

That left plenty of room for good writing and intellectual variety and experimentation. Squarely on mission, for example, was a set of tools to help readers choose their "next book," including a page that served as a gateway to lists of recommended Jewish reading, organized into various themes. A "Sense of Place" list, for example, featured books with especially detailed treatments of locales. Another, labeled "Struggle and Justice," listed books that touched on politics, philosophy, and law. For readers looking for newly published work, one panel on the site's main page listed reviews from many sources. Visitors could search the entire Nextbook database, assembling their own, custom-made lists. Some of the available lists were keyed to Nextbook readings, lectures, and performances, thus providing a link between private reading and public events.

Still, the principle governing the website's content remained the one Mr. Fried and Mrs. Bernstein had set for it: being a "gateway" to Jewish literature and culture, with no "barriers to entry." As much as Mr. Eskin sought to give Nextbook.org a distinct personality, he was also determined not to let it become a megaphone for any particular point of view. He and his deputy, Sara Ivry, deliberately featured a broad range of topics and deliberately posted interviews, reviews, links, and freelance contributions that showcased opinions other than their own. Nextbook was not, Mr. Eskin insisted, a blog, nor would it become one. Still, he did not object when, in 2005, the newly created "Best of Blogs Awards" surprisingly named Nextbook as one of ten finalists in the "literary blog" category. A month later, after final balloting, the site went on to win that category outright.

By then, any doubts about the role of original content had been dispelled. The front page was redesigned to make more room for feature articles and reviews, with narrower columns for program links, book recommendations, and a daily digest of short cultural news items. For the first time, the home page contained a new designation, "Cover Story," to describe a much longer, in-depth kind of reporting. A typical front page in mid-2005 contained half a dozen articles, each with a different byline, only a small minority of which would normally bear the name of a Nextbook employee. The topics ranged from winking observations on pop culture (two pieces delved into celebrity casting controversies in the Broadway revival of *Fiddler on the Roof*) to serious writers meditating on serious writers (including an interview with Jonathan Rosen touching on Tolstoy and George Eliot, among others, and an obituary of Saul Bellow by David Mamet).

In keeping with the increasing popularity of multimedia content on the web, Nextbook.org began posting recordings of its interviews and some video and audio from Nextbook's live programs in Chicago, Washington, and Seattle. The next step, as Mr. Eskin saw it, should be to launch a podcast—a medium that was still in its infancy in 2005. (The name refers to Apple's iPod, on which most podcasts were then meant to be heard. The first iPod had been released only three years earlier. The first self-described podcast appeared in mid-2004.) Like most Americans at the time, Ms. Sandorf, Mrs. Bernstein, and Mr. Fried had no idea what a podcast was, much less how it would add to the offerings on the site. But Mr. Eskin's enthusiasm for the idea was infectious, and the cost was small—around $10,000. "Our aim," he explained to the Keshet trustees in early 2005, "is to develop a lively, eclectic show that would be rich in content similar to—and, whenever possible, adapted from—Nextbook's other projects: the website, the publishing series, and the public programs."

As with the launch of the website itself, Mrs. Bernstein and Mr. Fried continued to view this next stage of evolution as low-cost, low-risk, and possibly high-return. The pilot Nextbook podcast appeared on the Web site in mid-June 2005, featuring a ten-minute interview about the 20th century Ukrainian-Jewish writer Dovid Bergelson. It was primitive in some respects and was posted without much fanfare, more a test of the form than the unveiling of a proud new feature. Later productions were more polished, with the addition of music and multiple voices, including a regular host, Laurel Snyder, a journalist and blogger based in Atlanta. The next step was to develop the form into a full half-hour audio program.

The website was blossoming, and word-of-mouth seemed to be spreading. People who spoke to Ms. Sandorf, Mr. Eskin, or to the Keren Keshet trustees described the site in all the ways they had hoped to hear: attractive, lively, thoughtful, smart, and deeply Jewish. But what Mr. Fried and Mrs. Bernstein really wanted to know—and so did everyone at Nextbook—was how many people they were reaching, how those people were using the site's various features, what potential audience were they not yet reaching, and what would it take to draw in those additional users. To these questions, the answers were frustratingly vague and debatable.

The tracking and measurement of Internet audiences was then a new and highly imprecise business. Such precision as was available usually came at high cost, not only in money but in technical demands on the site and its users. (Requiring readers to register before entering the site, for example, could produce plenty of information, but would also make the site cumbersome to use and probably discourage people from visiting.) In its early years, Nextbook.org relied on a fairly basic program for counting visitors, called a log analyzer, whose results were not altogether reliable nor especially descriptive. But they hoped it would at least be a good indicator of trends—steadily rising numbers of visits, page views, and e-mail subscribers surely meant that something good was happening, even if it was difficult to know exactly what.

In 2006, based on the log analyzer, Nextbook.org seemed to be averaging 19,000 visits per week and 40,000 page views—suggesting that the average viewer was opening two pages per visit. It seemed that the site was managing to serve its essential literary mission, given that well over one-third of the viewed pages were in the book section, and book sales through the site were sharply up. If the upward trends in the data were true, one reason might well have been that Nextbook was regularly paying for ads on the major search engines, so that a link to Nextbook.org would appear when someone searched for a prominent Jewish author. If you entered "Philip Roth," "Saul Bellow," or "Anne Frank" in a Yahoo or Google search, one of the "sponsored" entries on the right side of the screen would be a link to the Nextbook website and its articles and listings for that author. (It's worth noting that this kind of marketing was essentially a high-tech variation on the earliest idea behind Nextbook: a means by which someone seeking a Jewish book or author might find immediate guidance to other, similar books, and to other Jewish topics and ideas.) Other ads appeared in the online version of major periodicals popular with Jewish readers, such as *Ha'aretz, The New Republic,* and *Atlantic Online.*

———

On July 1, 2004, what had been the Nextbook "project," an activity sheltered entirely within Keren Keshet, became Nextbook, Inc., a separately incorporated nonprofit organization with a budget of roughly $4 million. With the new incorporation came an independent board, on which sat Mem Bernstein and Arthur Fried, alongside four other members who had all, at various points, consulted on the design and construction of the project: Eli Evans, an author and president emeritus of the Charles H. Revson Foundation; radio documentarian David Isay; and writer and critic Judith Shulevitz. The staff had moved from a cramped, temporary space on West 80th Street to brighter, roomier quarters in SoHo.

By this time, the organization was running public programs, with local staff and a roster of regular venues, in all three cities. Programs were branching well outside the libraries that were originally supposed to be their primary sponsors and facilitators. Readings, book clubs, and lectures were taking place at bars and cafes, among other less-formal settings, luring audiences that weren't denizens of the library and were, to some extent, newer to the cities' cultural milieu than were regular patrons in libraries.

One regular participant at Nextbook events in a Chicago pub told an interviewer in 2004, "The thought that you can come out after work, get a beer or maybe something to eat, and hear a good, challenging literary talk is really appealing—in a way that a lecture at the downtown library never would be. I like lectures, I like good books, I'm interested in Jewish authors. But I'm just not going to go to the [downtown] library after work, pay for a parking space, and sit around in a tight chair for two hours in my suit."

The Jewish literary world in all three cities was taking notice, and the combination of high literary standards and Jewish particularity was winning plaudits. One example: After a Nextbook lecture by Pulitzer Prize-winning author Michael Chabon in Seattle, the editor and critic Christopher Frizzelle wrote in the independent local periodical *The Stranger* that "one got the sense that one was being let in on a side of Chabon's work/life/art that only the context of a Jewish audience, and the financial support of a Jewish institution, could have coaxed out of him." A Nextbook event, he wrote, "never had an exclusionary vibe to it, and was marketed to the mainstream. In contrast to small bookstore readings or Seattle Arts & Lectures' giant hall, Nextbook's readings and onstage interviews (more than a dozen a year) often happened in bars."[28]

While happy with the non-"exclusionary" vibe, Mr. Fried, Mrs. Bernstein, and Ms. Sandorf kept a careful eye on the balance between trendy events and venues on the one hand and serious, challenging content on the other. "We want to be provocative," one staff member working on public programs said, "but not provocative for its own sake." The desire to reach bigger, newer audiences—people who are not already steeped in Jewish literature and may not even know whether they are interested in it—pulled somewhat against the desire to draw people into a deeper relationship to the ideas, topics, and texts that Nextbook was meant to showcase.

For all the creativity and marketing that went into them, the events often drew audiences that were smaller than expected—from a high of 300 to 500 people for approximately a half-dozen high-profile events to lows of 40 or fewer for an equal number of others. In 2005, average attendance was 148 for the headliner Writer's Series, which took place in larger venues, 146 for the offbeat Readings and Performances that more often went on in bars and cafes, and 75 for the more scholarly History, Culture, and Ideas series, which consisted of fairly traditional lectures. Most of these numbers were below the projections that Ms. Sandorf had presented to her board at the beginning of the year, though the trendy Readings and Performances did slightly better than originally projected.

Mr. Fried and Mrs. Bernstein were inclined to be patient, recognizing that the whole menu of public offerings was still new and most of it remained experimental. Still, these activities were expensive to produce, considering the fees paid to authors and speakers, the rental costs of many venues, the price of advertising and program materials, and the salaries of staff who kept it all running in three cities. It was clear, for example, that the best audience numbers corresponded to the best-known, and thus most expensive, speakers. It didn't help that some of these more-famous personalities, although they were Jewish, had distinguished themselves more as general literary figures than as writers about Judaism. The risk that Keren Keshet might come to regard the program as merely "Jewish Lite," as Mr. Fried put it, was never far from staff members' minds.

Ms. Sandorf and her team understood that a cost-benefit reckoning would come at some point. Yet every attempt to present more probing, more deeply Jewish programming seemed to lead to dwindling attendance; efforts to shore up attendance with spicier topics and better-known talent seemed to skate dangerously close to "Jewish lite." So in 2004 and '05, they sought to broaden their base and share more of the responsibility of creating programs and reading groups with more libraries across the country. In a partnership with the American Library Association, Nextbook issued a nationwide Request for Proposals in which libraries could win a small grant, along with some training and logistical help, to sponsor a series of readings and discussions on substantive Jewish themes. The applicants would have to recruit a well-qualified discussion leader; provide a suitable location; organize, staff and promote the events; and describe what results it expected to achieve. Nearly 70 libraries spanning 29 states won grants of $1,500 each, plus organizing help from Nextbook staff.

The results were impressive—substantive, well-attended, often creatively run—and their reach was considerably wider than could be achieved in just the three Nextbook pilot cities. The idea was something akin to franchising: creating a standard, quality product that others could deliver with some financial and technical support, but without the direct expense of deploying staff and mounting programs in-house. It seemed well suited to extend beyond libraries to other local organizations that might want to promote Jewish literature or create opportunities for Jewish residents to gather, learn, and network. Because the grants were awarded competitively, quality and cost control were built into the model. The idea gathered steam quickly, at first under the heading "Nextbook in . . ." (as in "Nextbook in Miami" or "Nextbook in Pittsburgh") and later more simply named "Nextbook Festivals."

As another year passed, and audience numbers in the three pilot cities continued to be disappointing, Mr. Fried and Mrs. Bernstein found themselves increasingly disenchanted with the costly in-house programs and drawn more and more to the franchising model. The search for additional partners to host Nextbook-inspired programs—synagogues? Jewish Community Centers? other Jewish cultural or religious organizations?—gained strength in 2006, and a few tentative agreements for jointly sponsored local programming led to a spate of pilot projects.

In early 2007, however, Julie Sandorf stepped down as CEO of Nextbook, and her departure set off a new reckoning with costs, benefits, and priorities. She had been offered a choice position in American Jewish philanthropy, the presidency of the Charles H. Revson

Foundation, and she chose not to let the opportunity pass her by*. But one result of her departure was that the local programs, both directly run and franchised, lost their keenest advocate. Before long, as Ms. Sandorf was preparing to pass the baton to new leadership, Mrs. Bernstein and Mr. Fried were becoming more and more skeptical that the model could produce transformative results, and concern about its cost was taking center stage. Attempts at forging partnerships to mount "Nextbook Festivals" continued for another year or two, though not backed by great confidence or enthusiasm within the organization. Nor did the local partners exhibit much passion for the idea or advance any strong argument for continuing it. By late 2008, when the international financial collapse took a giant bite out of the foundation's assets, the cost was becoming harder to justify. In 2010, Mr. Fried and Mrs. Bernstein decided it was time to bring the programs to an end.

One area in which there was no hint of "Jewish Lite" was the Jewish Encounters book series, where Jonathan Rosen was assembling a pantheon of distinguished Jewish authors to write books on history's most important Jewish thinkers, leaders, and issues. In 2005, the first two titles appeared and immediately set a tone for the series, striking precisely the balance that had been so elusive in the public programs and lectures: serious, penetrating writing about important Jewish subjects, yet wrapped in an inviting, non-academic style that appealed to a broad readership.

---

* Among Ms. Sandorf's signature initiatives as head of the Revson Foundation was a nationally celebrated program to strengthen neighborhood libraries across New York City, where the foundation is headquartered. She attributes her understanding of the value of libraries to her experience at Nextbook and the influence of Mem Bernstein and Arthur Fried.

The first of these was *The Life of David*, a biography of the poet-king by the celebrated poet and essayist Robert Pinsky. Next came *Maimonides*, a lyrical appreciation of the Torah scholar, philosopher, and physician written by surgeon and bioethicist Serwin B. Nuland. Dr. Nuland had become internationally famous for an earlier book, *How We Die*, on the physical experience of approaching the end of life, which won the National Book Award for nonfiction. The publisher, Pantheon/Schocken, made the two books the literal center-piece of its fall catalogue and marketed them vigorously. Nextbook, too, mounted an ambitious marketing campaign, relying partly on mailing lists from organizations like the National Association of Jews and Medicine and the Jewish Studies Association, and partly on print ads in major periodicals. A stream of new titles followed quickly, including biographies, histories, and meditations on themes and cultural phenomena in Jewish history.

Nextbook's Jewish Encounters series was not just a collection of important writing by important Jewish writers. It was, as Mr. Rosen had envisioned, a more personal and emotional—and very Jewish—kind of exposition: a dialogue of sorts, between the author and subject, between past and present, as if *b'chavruta*, a classic yeshiva study technique in which a pair of seekers read, examine, and debate texts and issues together, over a common table. In Mr. Rosen's series, the authors did not merely research and report on their subjects, they entered and dwelt in, interrogated and responded to, the Jewish world those subjects inhabited. The resulting blend of intellectual and spiritual discovery was distinctive and rare, and Mr. Rosen took pains with each author to keep the work from veering too much in either direction. He chose the subjects first, then sought authors who he believed would engage with those topics in both analytical and personal ways.

As a result, Mr. Rosen's job—his relationship with his roster of authors—was often a mixture of the literary and the therapeutic. In his introduction to *Maimonides,* Dr. Nuland tells the story of experiencing a crisis of confidence midway through his research on the book, when he suddenly felt inadequate to tackle one of Judaism's most imposing thinkers, and unable to finish. "I cried out to Jonathan Rosen," he wrote, "the general editor of this new series of books on Jewish themes, when I for several months had been immersed in the deep, inky waters of the vast Maimonidean literature, . . . and begged to be relieved of a burden for which I had become certain that I was incompetent.

"But Jonathan would hear none of it. . . . There had been several reasons that I—rather than an acknowledged authority—had been chosen for this mission, he replied to my importunings. . . . Mainly what he was seeking, he explained, was an encounter between a contemporary observer and that towering figure from the Jewish past. Is there some common ground on which Rabbi Moses ben Maimon . . . can walk together with a man or woman of today? . . . Can we in our time recognize in him attributes we see in ourselves, or is he so removed from the experience of a present-day mind that we can only study him, but never comprehend fully who he was? 'If Maimonides is lost to you,' wrote Jonathan, 'then he is lost to all of us.' And with those words, I decided to become Everyman."

"The freakout factor is amazing," Mr. Rosen said sometime later, reflecting on similar incidents with other authors that arose after Dr. Nuland's inaugural attack of self-doubt. The unusual nature of the project—the personal, nearly autobiographical exposure to which it subjected its authors, as they confronted the monumental stature of their subjects—often made for a perplexing and intimidating assignment, even (perhaps especially) for the most distinguished writers.

"They're making an inner psychological journey," Mr. Rosen continued, "that's often amazingly fraught with doubt and self-criticism.
That's partly the nature of the task, breaking new ground in an unfamiliar form, and maybe it's part of the legacy of being an assimilated
American."

By the end of 2007, Mr. Rosen had more than 15 titles in some
stage of production, but the climate of books and publishing was
growing more hostile—not just for Nextbook, but for all book projects that were not destined to be blockbusters. Bookstores were closing across the country, sales were plummeting, and no less a cultural
arbiter than Apple founder Steve Jobs would soon proclaim, in early
2008, that "nobody reads books anymore." Amazon released its revo-
lutionary new e-reader, the Kindle, in November 2007, thrusting the
industry into an upheaval that in some ways never abated. "Publishing
is in a kind of crisis now," Mr. Rosen told the Nextbook board in late
2008. "The mood is very grim and stressed." He reported that Sonny
Mehta, head of the Knopf Group at Random House, which includes
Schocken, where the Jewish Encounter series was published, still
liked the series, but the company was constricting. Nextbook could
no longer expect the kind of marketing support the publisher had
been providing for the earliest titles. And it would have to make certain that the future work it produced sold well enough to preserve
Schocken's enthusiasm.

This would prove to be a struggle. By the end of 2009, an insight-
ful and elegantly written biography of 19th century British Prime
Minister Benjamin Disraeli, by the poet and journalist Adam Kirsch,
had sold barely 5,000 copies after nearly 18 months in print and a
favorable review in *The New York Times*. Other titles were doing a bit
better, but few had yet risen above four figures. Suddenly, the pressure
on the book series was beginning to resemble the one that had plagued

the public programs: Rich content would normally appeal to select but smaller audiences; the desire for a bigger market would be a temptation to lower the intellectual (and, worse, the Jewish) seriousness of the material.

As Mrs. Bernstein and Mr. Fried continued to ponder the cost-benefit calculation, their considerable pride in the Jewish Encounters book series increasingly clashed with their desire to reach more than a niche audience of Jewish literati. They cut the budget for book production in half at the end of 2010 and encouraged Mr. Rosen to make more aggressive use of his authors as promoters of their own work. They also pressed him to make the rounds of Jewish philanthropy in search of other contributors to the project, though the response he got was mostly small offers of support to promote individual titles. When Mr. Fried plaintively asked, at a board meeting in November 2010, "Is marketing books a Sisyphean task?" the future of publishing at Nextbook was becoming more and more doubtful.

Promisingly, the intensified marketing scheme soon began to pay off. *The Eichman Trial*, by historian Deborah Lipstadt, had gone into its sixth printing by the end of its first year; a book by poet Peter Cole and critic Adina Hoffman titled *Sacred Trash*, about ancient manuscripts and contemporary scholars, was in its fifth printing after a similar time on the market. The life of Spinoza, by the prominent philosopher and novelist Rebecca Goldstein, was approaching 30,000 copies and had taken on new life as a university textbook. A biography of Emma Lazarus by poet Esther Schor, after five years in print, had become the basis of an exhibit at the National Museum of American Jewish History and was enjoying brisk sales in the museum shop as well as online.

Nonetheless, for Mr. Fried and Mrs. Bernstein, the unease about costs and benefits, and their suspicion that the books were appealing only to an ultra-literate (and not necessarily Jewish) readership, had barely abated. By the end of 2013, Mr. Rosen had concluded that he would not be able to move the needle enough to overcome their reservations. He stepped down early the following year, although many of the books he had commissioned were still being finished, and they would continue to appear, with decreasing frequency, for half a dozen more years.

"It was very difficult to let this series end," Mrs. Bernstein said close to a decade later. "It was such a pleasure to sit at a table with Jonathan, to listen to how his mind works, and to see the fruits of all that effort. We were enjoying ourselves enormously, doing this. But we knew that financially we just couldn't keep it going. It couldn't be just something we enjoyed; we had to be reasonable. But still, it was sad."

Well before that decision was made, profound changes were taking place in the structure and mission of the Nextbook organization. Ms. Sandorf's departure had come to the Keshet trustees as a surprise, and they had given no thought to who else might lead the organization in her absence. Seeking a new CEO whom they could trust immediately—someone both entrepreneurial enough to pilot the business and mission-driven enough to focus intently on its core purposes—they turned to an old friend, Morton Landowne, a business executive who had devoted three decades to his manufacturing company and was ready, at age 60, for a change.

Over the course of more than 20 years as a member and lay leader at Lincoln Square Synagogue, Mr. Landowne had become close to Zalman and Mem Bernstein, and the two families had often shared meals and traveled together. Mr. Landowne was an astute follower of Jewish literature and culture and had a long resume in Jewish communal and religious life. Among other things, he had been president of Edah, the organization to promote Modern Orthodoxy founded by Rabbi Saul Berman, to which Keren Keshet had made several grants. The foundation trustees knew Mr. Landowne both personally and professionally; they had confidence in him both as a manager and as a believer in Nextbook's mission.

"Most of all," Mrs. Bernstein pointed out, "he was a culture maven. He read everything, saw everything, knew who was creating what. That was his world. That's where he belonged. And it was fun to work with him."

In fact, the trustees had already turned to Mr. Landowne a few times in the past to be their surrogate at Nextbook events they were unable to attend. In particular, his account of two "Nextbook Festival" events made a strong impression on them. Both programs, he told them, were of very high quality, well planned and executed, but the crowds were disappointing—not sparse, but not especially large either, and seemingly heavy with "regulars" who attended Jewish events often and were likely not discovering anything fundamentally new. Meanwhile, he couldn't help observing, the cost was high, relative to the apparent impact. This was exactly the kind of nuanced but clearheaded assessment they needed and valued.

Most of all, Mr. Landowne was someone whom they could trust, who shared their world view and values. That kind of relationship was more important at Nextbook than at almost any other grantee organization, because Mr. Fried and Mrs. Bernstein did not consider themselves merely as funders of Nextbook. "This was a venture capital operation," Mr. Fried said, "without the profit motive. It was a business, a multifaceted business, and we were the shareholders. We looked at ourselves not as funders, but as *owners of an enterprise*. And we did our best, using considerable funds at the time, to strengthen this enterprise in as many ways as we could, until we came to a transition point, where we wished to re-evaluate some of the things we were doing."

Although they had not sought a change in executive leadership and regretted Ms. Sandorf's departure, Mrs. Bernstein and Mr. Fried saw the transition as a good opportunity for re-evaluation and fresh thinking. If their "venture capital operation" lacked a profit motive, it nonetheless existed to generate a human return on the foundation's investment—specifically, a growing number of Jewish readers and seekers drawing nourishment from Jewish writing. Mr. Landowne was more than ready to take up that challenge, starting with an assessment of how Nextbook could boost its return on Keren Keshet's dollars.

By the time he stepped into the job, the decision to discontinue the public programs and library partnerships had already been taken, so Mr. Landowne started by reviewing the book series and the website. He saw, at that point, no reason to tinker with the former—he considered Mr. Rosen a "genius" and was impressed by the quality of the authors and topics he had lined up for publication. He pointed out the high costs of production relative to the sales volume, as Mr. Rosen had also done, but both men understood that the trustees were content, at the time, to let the series build steam and gradually gain a following. (Concerns about the cost-benefit problem didn't become acute for another year or two.) Instead, Mr. Landowne's principal questions were about the website, which he saw as having the greatest potential to reach significantly more people than it had thus far.

The quality of the writing and thought on the site, he knew, was exceptionally high. That had been due in large part to the editorial and technological talents of its founder, Blake Eskin. But those talents were becoming more and more widely coveted in the burgeoning marketplace for online journalism, and in 2006 no less than *The New Yorker* was reaching out to Mr. Eskin to become the first editor of its new website. When he accepted that offer, Mr. Fried, Mrs. Bernstein, and Ms. Sandorf felt his departure keenly, and Nextbook.org was still struggling to adjust by the time Mr. Landowne arrived on the scene. The staff had grown to encompass several talented writers and editors, who endeavored to operate the site more or less as Mr. Eskin had done.

The problem, as Mr. Landowne saw it, was similar to that of the public programs: A high-quality product was reaching too few people and was struggling to strike a balance between appealing to unaffiliated Jews—by not spotlighting Judaism and Jewish content so emphatically that it scared off the uninitiated—and satisfying a mission that demanded meaty, thought-provoking, thoroughly Jewish writing. Although the content was first-rate, in his view the *point* of the website, the essential reason a reader would want to return to it regularly and devote serious time to reading it, was not yet sufficiently in focus. Ambivalence about its Jewish identity was part of the problem, he felt. For example, he was surprised to hear from one editorial staff member that the word "Jewish" was banned in headlines. Another possible concern was the emphasis on cultural commentary above all—with almost no coverage of politics and little by way of lighter fare. The site had the feel of a topnotch cultural journal, perhaps akin to the *New York Review of Books*—a quality that nicely satisfied the desire for dignified writing about serious Jewish issues but did little to tempt a less intellectual readership.

Still, recognizing these concerns was not the same as knowing what to do about them. Mr. Landowne was a seasoned manager and, as an avid consumer of Jewish thought and writing, he was an excellent judge of content and thus a good proxy for at least one kind of

Nextbook customer. But he wasn't a journalist or editor or publisher (at least not yet), and he felt he needed someone with stellar credentials in those areas to help him decide whether and how to re-think Nextbook.org.

Luckily, some timely advice from an old friend supplied an answer. Ami Eden, who had until recently been executive editor and web editor of *The Forward,* told Mr. Landowne that yet another leadership struggle at that newspaper (similar to an earlier one that had led Jonathan Rosen to leave the paper and join Nextbook) had resulted in the departure of one of its star journalists, cultural editor Alana Newhouse. "She's a real talent," Mr. Eden told Mr. Landowne. "You should go after her." In a matter of days, he set up an interview over lunch.

The main course had barely arrived before Mr. Landowne knew this was exactly the person he was looking for. "Alana was a product of Jewish day school, all the way through 12th grade," he said. "She had a familiarity with a lived Jewish life. She spoke Hebrew. She was a graduate of the Columbia School of Journalism. She was a masterful writer, with an eye for what made something interesting and worth reading. She had spent seven years at *The Forward* and seemed to know everybody in Jewish culture, from Philip Roth on down. I left that meeting and said to myself, 'I have found my partner.'"

If Mr. Landowne was, as he put it, "smitten," Ms. Newhouse was not yet ready to say, "I do." She had joined *The Forward* not out of a desire to make a career in Jewish letters, but to gain experience, build a resume, and eventually move on to her first love, general-interest magazine journalism. What Mr. Landowne saw as the rich background of a "lived Jewish life" was beginning to feel to Ms. Newhouse like something intellectually stifling. The prospect of moving to yet another Jewish publication held little appeal for her. "I wanted to get away from all that, frankly—go to India, do yoga for a while. Anything but what I'd been doing." On the other hand, she had to admit there were pluses too, and she felt them tugging at her even as she tried to resist them.

One plus was Mr. Landowne himself, whom she immediately liked and from whom she got an appealing sense of intellectual adventure, wide-ranging curiosity, and camaraderie—all qualities she had felt lacking in her recent years at *The Forward*. Another attractive factor was the Nextbook website itself—not just its content, but its style. "The thing about Nextbook I remember appreciating profoundly was its commitment to aesthetics," she said several years later. "It was very, very lovely to look at. The design work on it was—well, it felt like a legitimately great American cultural brand." One thing she had found especially dispiriting about Jewish journalism and some corners of Jewish communal life was their utter lack of flair. That, she could tell, would not be a problem at Nextbook.

The problem for her was exactly the one that Mr. Landowne had zeroed in on when he first arrived: The essential purpose of the site, what marketing jargon would describe as its unique value proposition, was hard to discern. "You clearly respect your audience," she told Mr. Landowne over lunch, "and you want to create something beautiful and high class for them. But aside from that, I have no idea what you do. I can't figure it out. So I think I'm not the right person to come work for you."

If she had a hard time grasping what Nextbook did, she had no such uncertainties about what she wanted to do. Her next career move, she told Mr. Landowne, would be in journalism—not cultural essays and criticism, but actual reporting on unfolding events. "What I valued," she remembers telling him, "and what I felt was increasingly missing from Jewish life and the broader American society, were the mirrors that good journalism holds up to people—showing them their lives, the consequences of their choices, the opportunities they take and don't take. To me, this was quite different—indeed, the opposite—of the kind of top-down communal messaging that philanthropic outfits often supported, which, to my ears anyway, usually condescendingly demand that people believe X, Y, or Z." She wanted to work in the realm of information, not just ideas.

But to Mr. Landowne, those ambitions were exactly why she was the right person to come work at Nextbook. After another meeting or two, he had persuaded her at least to dip a toe in the water. "Try us," she remembers him saying. "What's the worst that could happen? Go to India afterward." She started in the summer of 2008, though with some lingering skepticism that the arrangement would work in the long run. "To be perfectly frank," she said, "I did not believe I would be there more than a year. Nor do I believe that anyone really thought it was going to work." Among other things, she reckoned, the kind of journalism she wanted to practice would be complicated, expensive, and messy—"you'll need libel lawyers and so on"—and she doubted that the foundation would have the patience or stamina for it in the long run.

Mr. Landowne, however, was sure it was going to work. To give Ms. Newhouse exactly the support she wanted, he even hired two of her former colleagues from *The Forward:* Wayne Hoffman to be managing editor, and Gabriel Sanders as business manager. (Both would still be in those positions a dozen years later.) The team set to work analyzing the content and the audience, assessing what was working and what not, and weighing alternative approaches to staffing and outsourcing.

For the Keshet trustees, the switch from Ms. Sandorf to Mr. Landowne and Ms. Newhouse was more than a change of personnel.

It also represented a fundamental shift in Nextbook's relationship to its audience and, ultimately, even an express change in its mission. Under Ms. Sandorf, daughter of a secular family, whose résumé had contained not one thing that said "Jewish," the organization had scrupulously adhered to the charge that Mrs. Bernstein and Mr. Fried had originally given it: to present an enticing selection of Jewish writing to a Jewish audience that need not have any emotional ties to Judaism. The desire to appeal to the unaffiliated, and even to the disaffected, kept Ms. Sandorf and her team on a strategic tightrope, careful not to demand too much Jewish commitment from her audience while also not tipping in the other direction, toward a superficial "Jewish Lite."

By contrast, Mr. Landowne and Ms. Newhouse had résumés that practically pealed "Jewish." In his work with Edah and Lincoln Square Synagogue, and hers with *The Forward,* they were accustomed to addressing Jewish messages to Jewish audiences and relatively untroubled by the risk of alienating people for whom "Jewish" was a loaded word. They weren't convinced that the tightrope was walkable; in fact, they believed that trying to maintain this complex balance was the main reason why the essential point of Nextbook had never come into complete focus. Mr. Landowne and Ms. Newhouse wanted to address great Jewish writing to inquiring Jewish readers, regardless of their level of observance or education or experience—just people curious about Judaism and Jewishness. They wanted to answer Jewish questions with Jewish knowledge, thought, and commentary. People who avoided anything that seemed "too Jewish" were probably unreachable by a project like this—or, at a minimum, they were reachable only at too great a cost and too high a risk of failure.

By the end of 2008, the project's new leaders had persuaded Mr. Fried and Mrs. Bernstein that a more narrowly focused set of goals would be both more achievable and more strategically coherent. Henceforth, Nextbook would no longer strive to be "all things to all Jews." Instead, a new mission statement emphasized serving people who already have a desire for Jewish learning and are actively seeking ways to satisfy that desire. Reaching what Mr. Fried described as "the outermost ring" of Jewish society was now recognized as the "most elusive" of goals—still worth pursuing, if a good opportunity arose, but less urgent, and less likely to succeed, than "to engage those already engaged." As Mrs. Bernstein summed it up: "We don't have to reach all that far to reach out."

─────────

As Ms. Newhouse delved deeper into the operation and performance of the Nextbook website, she gradually reached three related conclusions. The first was that traffic to the site was not in fact as robust as had been previously thought. At the time Nextbook.org was created, methods of gauging readership were relatively primitive. Managers and editors had been relying on an early, very basic program for counting visitors called a log analyzer, whose results were at best useful for following trends over time, but not for ascertaining the actual number of visitors or page views on any given day. Google Analytics, a much more reliable way of counting users and tracking the amount of time they spend on the site, had come on the market only at the end of 2005. Less than three years later, when analysts applied it to Nextbook.org, the results were sharply lower than those from the log analyzer. The site was not casting nearly as wide a net as it had seemed.

Her second observation was that the website was not posting enough new material fast enough, on sufficiently timely subjects, to make a reader feel a need to check it daily or even weekly. It was publishing three to five original pieces a week of 3,000 to 5,000

words, plus smaller items like brief reviews or commentary on linked
material. If the team were more like a newsroom than a cultural
website, with full-time reporters and editors and a stable of freelance
journalists, Ms. Newhouse believed the result would attract more
frequent visits. Better still, the live reporting and original articles
might entice other websites to comment on or link to them.

Of course, reporting on current events would mean publishing
articles that wander into controversial territory, probably including
some coverage of politics. That would violate what had been an un-
written but firm rule, and Ms. Newhouse had no idea how Mr. Fried
and Mrs. Bernstein would react to it. Ms. Sandorf had entertained
similar notions in the past but had been convinced that political content would not pass muster with the trustees. But Ms. Newhouse did
not consider this choice debatable, if the goal was to attract more
eyeballs to the site and stir up readers' enthusiasm and loyalty. "You
cannot have a magazine that attempts to address Jewish identity and
doesn't talk about religion or politics," she told Mr. Landowne at their
first meeting. "It doesn't make any sense to me."

Ms. Newhouse also believed that the coverage needed to appeal to
a all aspects of readers' lives, with a mix of different types and styles
of coverage that spanned, in her words, "high, low, and middle brow."
Although Mr. Landowne shared her strategic view for the site, he
warned her that any reference to "low-brow" writing—or possibly
even middle-brow—was sure to be a non-starter with the trustees.
This whole discussion about changing the scope and tenor of the
website's content would have to be broached carefully.

Ms. Newhouse's third, and in some ways most unsettling, conclusion was that the name "Nextbook" no longer bore any relationship
to the website and its contents—and bore even less relationship to the
kind of daily journalism she hoped to produce. Nextbook.org was no

longer about choosing one's "next book"—or any book at all, necessarily. It swept far more broadly over the Jewish cultural world. And
once the site started to present more daily news and features, it would
lose even more of its connection to finding a next book. The whole
book-finding idea was rooted in the original concept of libraries, librarians, and promoting published texts. As matters stood, and as
they were about to evolve, the name "Nextbook" was becoming jar-
ringly off-topic—like creating a website about cooking and calling it
"Choose a Refrigerator."

That conclusion may have struck Ms. Newhouse as merely logical,
but Mr. Landowne recognized it immediately as a minefield. Amend-
ing the mission had been fraught enough—requiring, as it did, that
Mrs. Bernstein and Mr. Fried relegate some of their original, cherished goals to a back burner. Tackling lighter and more political topics was sure to set off alarm bells, too. But changing the *name*—a
carefully cultivated brand, developed and polished at a cost of hundreds of thousands of dollars for research, design, and production—
would be a far more unnerving step to take.

Throughout the late months of 2008, Mr. Landowne took on the
delicate mission of unfurling these new ideas—slowly, diplomatically,
and with a solid buttress of evidence and reasoning—for Mrs. Bernstein and Mr. Fried. Their initial skepticism wore away bit by bit,
without disappearing altogether. By the time Ms. Newhouse presented her ideas at the end of the year, the trustees had come to accept
the altered vision as well-thought-out and worth trying, even if the
danger of taking it too far still troubled them.

As Mr. Landowne had expected, the search for a new name gener-
ated the most debate and unease. So here, too, he took pains to prepare the ground with an open, deliberative process. The new name,
he explained, would need to be both dignified and simple; it would

need to convey responsibility and reliability without seeming pompous; and it would need to point, at least obliquely, to Jewish roots. One early idea was "Scroll," though that felt a bit antiquarian. "Tablet," another strong contender, struck everyone as stronger—more solid, more authoritative, but also (unlike a lengthy scroll) succinct and easy to read. It would not be the only *Tablet* in publication—the Catholic Church had at least two small periodicals by that name—but it would be the only general-interest web magazine called *Tablet*. Despite some anxiety about a Jewish news site sharing a name with a Catholic masthead—Mr. Fried, in particular, had grown up in Brooklyn, where he remembered *The Tablet* as the diocesan newsletter—the name still had more advantages than any other under consideration.

By early 2009, what Mr. Landowne described as a "massive site redesign" was in progress, under the new working title of *Tablet*, with the provocative tag line, "Making, Breaking, and Remaking Jewish Culture." (That proved to be a provocation too far; by the time the new site launched, it had been softened to "A New Read on Jewish Life.") A re-envisioned blog section and news digest would now be known as "The Scroll"—a context that made the word less suggestive of sacred parchment and more of a constantly rolling stream of information. Editorial staff would now be expected to file at least two or three new stories a week, with the rest coming from a team of freelancers Ms. Newhouse was busy recruiting. The goal, she told the trustees, would be to become "*the* address for Jewish culture with CNN, NPR, and the New York Times" at least as much as with the loftier cultural outlets. Besides some basic logistical steps, like registering the new domain name and optimizing the content so that it would appear in search engines like Google, the site's architecture would also have to be totally re-engineered to accommodate the higher volume of new stories, graphics, and blog posts projected to go online hour by hour.

In April 2009, Nextbook.org went dark. In June, *Tablet* was born. "This is a big deal for the magazine," Mr. Fried said at the start of the transition. "Expansion, changing focus, a redo of the website—it's a new beginning. And I hope it works."

———

It worked. The first issues of *Tablet* were not a radical departure from the earlier Nextbook website, but the articles were more numerous, ranging more widely across the cultural landscape with a greater variety of styles and levels of sophistication. The site was still more a cultural magazine than a newspaper—most articles were what Ms. Newhouse described as "contemplative, long pieces," just as they had been under Nextbook. But they appeared more frequently, and they touched on controversial themes involving things like U.S.-Israel relations, varieties and manifestations of anti-Semitism, and some of the internecine cultural and generational tensions in American Jewry. The inaugural issue contained, for the first time, a section called "News and Politics," with an article by the conservative journalist Seth Lipsky comparing the Israel policies of Presidents George W. Bush and Barack Obama, and a reflection on America's relations with Iran by the Iranian-Jewish writer Roya Hakakian.

From a more left-leaning perspective, the site also touted as a regular columnist Victor Navasky, the legendary editor of *The Nation*, and included on its staff Liel Leibovitz, a young, Israeli-born journalist who had made waves in Jewish journalism for what were then his left-wing politics and criticism of the Jewish state. (His political views would change profoundly in the coming years.) The new section, indeed the whole publication, was aiming to be, as Newhouse put it, "an exercise in heterodoxy—political, religious, cultural."

Elsewhere in *Tablet* were sections on Arts & Culture and on Life & Religion, containing the sorts of things that the Nextbook website would also have been happy to run—just more of them. The first issue offered a celebration of Yiddish theater, a number of reviews covering books by Jewish authors, and an excerpt from the latest book in the Nextbook "Jewish Encounters" series: Melvin Konner's *The Jewish Body*, about Judaism's effects on physical health, appearance, and well-being through the centuries. At this stage, *Tablet* was not yet a place to visit for breaking news or investigative reporting, but it supplied what Ms. Newhouse envisioned as a deeper, "analytic or mediating" treatment of current topics and events that would appeal to a thoughtful—or even just curious—Jewish reader. In its first two years, it won back-to-back National Magazine awards.

Boosted by some advertising in the Jewish press and online media, *Tablet's* faster pace and wider mix of stories quickly found an audience, which grew steadily during the initial year of publication. In the year before it shut down, Nexbook.org had been drawing just under 200,000 unique visitors a month. In December 2009, when Tablet was six months old, its readership was already more than triple that number, and by its first birthday it was being read on close to a million devices. Two years later, that number had tripled again and continued to grow sharply.

The wider range of stories not only crossed over into the once-taboo realms of politics and religion, but it ended up touching on topics that were not quintessentially or obviously Jewish. For example, articles on contemporary issues from the worlds of business and economics, travel, or general trends in American arts and letters, despite their Jewish bylines or protagonists, might not immediately seem relevant to Keren Keshet's original goal of enticing Jewish readers to read Jewish writing about Judaism. "Often," Ms. Newhouse said, "Arthur would send me links to articles and say, 'How does this fit into the definition of Jewish culture?' But I was interested more in identity than culture."

Her goal, in other words, was not solely to enrich someone's understanding of cultural Judaism, but to create an environment where Jewish visitors felt more Jewish, felt more a part of a Jewish community of readers and thinkers and explorers. The most popular sites, bloggers and influencers have found, are not those that merely present interesting information; they are the sites that create a feeling of *belonging*, of common purpose and shared experience. The Judaism of *Tablet*, in Ms. Newhouse's and Mr. Landowne's view, didn't inhere just in the Jewish content of this story or that story; it was in the atmosphere of Tablet's overall coverage, in which Jewish perspectives, values, history, and contemporary experiences were applied in multiple different ways to the vital topics of the day. She likened Tablet to a Shabbat table: "Every topic discussed doesn't have to be technically and squarely about Jews or Jewishness, but the setting and atmosphere would be obviously and importantly Jewish."

To achieve that ambition, publishing a lively, thoughtful cultural magazine, keeping it current, and weaving together a wide range of topics and styles seemed more than sufficient. Ms. Newhouse and her staff were not yet thinking of their product as a newspaper or aiming to turn it into one. They were specializing, at most, in what newspaper journalists call "second-day" stories: the articles that explain the background, causes and implications of events that had burst on the scene as "breaking" news the day before.

"I think of newspapers as hot media," she explained. "You're supposed to read something in the newspaper, throw it down on your kitchen table, and then go do something about it. Go out and vote, or write a letter to your member of Congress, or speak up at a school board meeting, or just go in to work and have a debate at the water cooler. But magazines are cool media. They're contemplative. They're meant to maybe change your mind, or enrich your mind, or bring definition and depth to the way you engage with the world. At the time, we saw *Tablet* as a magazine, and that was where we wanted to be. There were plenty of places to get Jewish *news*, but there weren't the analytic or mediating outlets that would help people *make sense* of the news they were reading."

But that world was changing. By 2009, long-smoldering problems in the newspaper industry had grown into a wildfire, with the financial collapse of 2008 having shredded the business model of newspapers of all kinds, nationwide. Advertising revenue, the loyalty of readers, and shareholders' tolerance of meager profits all were evaporating. Newsrooms were emptying out, and talented journalists with decades of accumulated expertise and contacts were suddenly unemployed. The idea that there would still be "plenty of places to get Jewish news" was becoming increasingly doubtful. Even the best "second-day" analytic pieces would do little good if no one was publishing the "first-day" stories.

Within a couple of years after its launch, Ms. Newhouse was convinced that *Tablet* would have to weave in elements of a newspaper, digging for events and running "hot" stories as well as reflecting more coolly on their meaning. Given the armies of gifted Jewish journalists available for freelance work, the idea was no longer farfetched. The talent was practically waiting at the door; the need was obvious and deepening; and the opportunity to bring Jewish news, features, and commentary to Jewish readers in a single place—one that could become an indispensable community for Jews seeking a Jewish understanding of the world around them—was becoming all but irresistible.

Better still, this time, the prospect of further expanding *Tablet*'s mission no longer faced serious skepticism from Mr. Fried and Mrs. Bernstein. The success of the redesigned magazine—traffic was approaching 2 million pageviews a month by the end of 2013, with sharp increases in the amount of time readers spent on site and the number who visited multiple times per month—made them confident that a further expansion of the mission would not only be feasible but wise.

Slowly at first, then more intensely, *Tablet* bylines began to resemble those of the better daily newspapers of the prior decade. Stories were increasingly current and new—not commentary on previously reported issues, but a regular serving of fresh reporting and information available only in *Tablet*. Reporters were pitching and submitting articles that in earlier years would have been considered competitive coups in commercial dailies. Other news outlets occasionally found themselves publishing stories based on revelations that originally appeared in *Tablet*.

Among the most widely noted of these was a lead story by freelancer Leah McSweeney and *Tablet* editor Jacob Siegel, exposing virulent anti-Semitism in the leadership of the Women's March, a protest movement reacting to the election of Donald Trump as president. Articles in other outlets, including Vox, the Daily Beast, and Business Insider, quickly picked up the story, citing *Tablet* as their source. Two weeks later, *The New York Times* ran its own version, crediting *Tablet* and recapitulating, in briefer form, most of the evidence first reported by Ms. McSweeney and Mr. Siegel. A week or two later, NBC News and Forbes magazine followed suit. For months, the story reverberated across the journalistic firmament and in the echo chambers of social media. Besides providing a giant lift to *Tab-*

let's national reputation, it drew the attention of a mass audience to an important Jewish issue that even other Jewish publications might never have discovered.

Other cases of deep, original reporting made a similar impact on the way both Jewish and general audiences learned about Jewish news. A detailed exposé on rising anti-Semitism in France ran in 2014 to fairly limited notice. But a few months later, when terrorists attacked a kosher supermarket in Paris, killing five people, *Tablet* re-ran the original story, which instantly became one of its best-read pieces of the year and influenced other reporting on the incident worldwide. A backgrounder on how news coverage frequently distorts reality in the Middle East, published in the midst of the 2014 Gaza war, drew 330,000 page views in a single day. Soon thereafter, *New York* magazine described *Tablet* as "the must-read for all young politically and culturally engaged Jews."

In well under a decade of its new incarnation, *Tablet* was proving itself to be not only authentically Jewish, authoritative, and informative, but something even more valuable: It had become essential reading. It had become important.

———

At least one element of Tablet's rapid success was in some ways a legacy of the Nextbook website that preceded it: the podcast of Jewish culture that Blake Eskin had pioneered at a time when most people hadn't yet even heard the word "podcast." That early experiment fared poorly in the transition from Nextbook.org to *Tablet*—the audio feature seemed too expensive and difficult to maintain at a time when the whole site was being re-conceived and re-engineered. Besides, after Mr. Eskin left Nextbook, the programming had lost a bit of its sparkle. But it had planted the idea that a podcast might attract an audience of its own and provide a vehicle for a distinctive kind of original content. Listening, it seemed reasonable to believe, could deepen the sense of belonging that Ms. Newhouse was hoping to engender, and might expand that communal feeling to people who would not otherwise spend hours a week reading online journalism.

The resurrected podcast was the brainchild of Tablet editors Liel Leibovitz, Stephanie Butnick, and Mark Oppenheimer. Their idea, responding to the increasingly combative tenor of political discourse in the late 20-teens, was, as Ms. Newhouse recalls it, "based on the idea that people can have conversations about anything with people who think differently from them. So, they said, we three are very different people. We come at issues of the news, of Jewish life and Jewish identity, from very different places. And we want a model for people to have a conversation—not a debate, not a tit for tat, but just a conversation—and walk away still respecting and maybe even loving each other."

It was an appealing idea, perfectly suited to the provocative but ideologically diverse contents of the website. Besides, the three editors added, it had a crucial selling point for Mrs. Bernstein and Mr. Fried: "It will be pretty inexpensive."

The new podcast, dubbed "Unorthodox," was a nearly instant success and soon began to draw a following all its own. The technology and aesthetics of podcasting had progressed markedly since the early Nextbook days, and the "Unorthodox" team took full advantage of the production and distribution mechanisms that were now available to them. The results were explosive.

From the original concept of simply presenting conversations among the three editors and invited guests, "Unorthodox" soon branched out to include recorded public events with a live audience. Before long, the popularity of these experiences led Jewish organizations and venues to ask to host "Unorthodox" broadcasts, which became "happenings" in Jewish communities all across the country. In just a few years, "Unorthodox" had managed to resurrect two of the original concepts behind Nextbook—public programs and online conversation—in a new, more practical format, with all the activities woven together into a single operation. And instead of Keren Keshet paying to host the public programs, the local sponsors were picking up a good part of the tab.

By that time, however, the idea was no longer "pretty inexpensive." After about 18 months of growth and refinement, the podcast's rising profile and the technical demands of recording live events clearly demanded better equipment, a professional producer, and higher-end guests. But those added costs were now much easier to justify, given the size and quality of the audiences "Unorthodox" was drawing: It had become by far the most popular Jewish podcast on iTunes, with more than 4 million downloads.

The whole "Unorthodox" experience, Ms. Newhouse believes, was the result of an atmosphere of imagination and experimentation—she calls it an "idea incubator"—that she cultivated, with Mrs. Bernstein's and Mr. Fried's encouragement, among the staff and freelancers of the *Tablet* community. It was, in many ways, the same kind of "design it, test it, learn from it" culture with which Julie Sandorf had begun in the earliest days of Nextbook. Under both regimes, Ms. Newhouse believes, the fertility of this creative atmosphere arose directly from the venturesome spirit of *Tablet*'s "owners."

"Mem and Arthur allowed me to privately incubate," she said in a 2021 interview. She had the luxury—rare in the world of foundation-funded projects—of a substantial, usually six-figure discretionary fund from which she could test new ideas largely on her own initiative. "I never had to report to them on the ideas we were trying out or justify what we did, unless it was going to turn into something big. And that was a good thing, because, half the time, the justification wasn't anything other than 'a smart person had an instinct.' A more formal or rigid kind of management might have made demands of me that would have closed off that kind of experimentation. We had a kind of latitude that's really unusual."

———

The website's growing success—whether measured by the number of unique visitors, or by influence on other news outlets, or by the inherent quality of the reporting and writing—drew more and more inquiry from Mr. Fried and Mrs. Bernstein about where else the accelerating momentum might lead. Some of the answers to that question pointed the way to new projects and features, with expanding audiences and new ways of appealing to them. But a few fell flat. For example, in 2010, following what Ms. Newhouse perceived to be the trustees' appetite for "the next new thing," she proposed creating a quarterly print edition of *Tablet*, available only by paid subscription, separate from and more in-depth than the online version. She developed the concept with a former executive of the magazine publisher Hachette Filipachi who served as the project's prime architect.

The idea was, by the standards of conventional wisdom, completely counterintuitive. At a time when publishers and purveyors of information were concluding that the future lay entirely online, and that ink on paper was headed for extinction, Ms. Newhouse was proposing to build a whole new print enterprise. What's more, she saw it appealing not primarily to traditionalists, but to younger audiences that, she believed, were once again warming to hard-copy publications and would pay $40 a year for a physical magazine that offered a more elite, sophisticated take on Jewish news and culture. The prospect of a fresh revenue stream obviously had its own appeal, as did the possibility of creating something that would forge a deeper, more personal relationship with readers than is typical online.

The print edition of *Tablet* survived barely more than a year—not long enough to test the idea that a physical publication might eventually appeal to a younger demographic, but more than long enough to demonstrate that, in the near term, the magazine was not expanding Tablet's already-strong market. The subscription revenue never came close to the forecasts of the publishing executive who helped conceive it. The print run was just 7,000 copies per issue, down from an initial projection of 20,000, and yet even so, thousands of copies went undistributed. "It was editorially fascinating and gorgeous, and it was just, overall, a beautiful magazine," Ms. Newhouse said. "But from either a business perspective or a mission perspective, it made no sense. It was serving a subset of Tablet's readership that we were already serving online. We were giving them a second dessert—which is great, if money is no object. But there was no way that this was the best use of anyone's resources."

Far more successful were two other new projects taken up at about the same time. The first was the establishment of an investigative reporting unit—the ultimate step in transforming the website from a cultural magazine to a full online newspaper. The spectacular impact of the Women's March story was among *Tablet*'s early achievements under its investigative banner, and a stream of other penetrating original reports on topics from Israel to academia to anti-Semitic attacks in Brooklyn followed.

The other new line of work bore a superficial resemblance to an old line of work: book publishing. But this time, instead of literary biographies, the titles would build on *Tablet*'s strengths as a source of offbeat information and lively writing. One early title was *The 100*

Most Jewish Foods, based on a special project that grew out of the magazine's Food section. Another was *The Newish Jewish Encyclopedia: From Abraham to Zabar's and Everything in Between,* by the same three editors who created "Unorthodox." *The Best of Tablet,* an anthology of articles from the past decade, was also planned.

The publisher of all these titles is Artisan Books, a division of Workman Publishing, which specializes in lifestyle and family books—a perfect niche for a series intended not as an intellectual dive into Jewish history but an enjoyable, occasionally irreverent introduction to the world of *Tablet.* By mid-2019, the food compilation was in its third printing with 40,000 copies distributed; it had already earned back its advance and was generating royalties. Other titles were meeting with enthusiastic critical reception and solid sales. The publishers told Ms. Newhouse that they considered the full roster strong enough that they saw no need for any significant marketing help from Tablet (apart from featuring the books on its website). "They see us as the content producers and themselves as the marketing,'" Ms. Newhouse told the trustees in 2019. So rather than shouldering the responsibility of selling the books, the website would benefit from Artisan's promotion of *Tablet* content.

For Mrs. Bernstein and Mr. Fried, the growth of *Tablet* was satisfying, encouraging, sometimes inspiring, but also expensive. Twenty years of contributions averaging $4 million a year represented a huge concentration of their philanthropy, rivaled only by the Jewish Community High School of the Bay. And as with the high school, the two trustees considered *Tablet*'s absolute dependence on their annual donations worrisome. Mr. Fried had originally envisioned a ten-year commitment to Nextbook. He had no regrets about extending that by another decade to give the new leadership team time to establish *Tablet* and grow it into something that other funders might be proud to support. But as the 20th anniversary of their first commitment was approaching, he and Mrs. Bernstein had begun warning Mr. Landowne and Ms. Newhouse that the spigot would not be open forever. New money—which could mean earned revenue but most likely meant new donors—would need to be found.

Yes, some earned revenue might help ease the pressure. But after several experiments with running ads in *Tablet*—which ended up cheapening the website's appearance without bringing in much money—the prospect of funding any significant part of the budget with revenue from advertising seemed a non-starter. The other standard means of earning money from an online publication was charging for subscriptions. But that would undermine the whole reason *Tablet* existed—to entice Jewish readers into a shared experience of learning and community with, in Mr. Fried's phrase, "no barriers to entry." Both the trustees and the site's managers reluctantly concluded that they would not be able to earn their way to independence.

So the solution lay in philanthropy, and in a campaign of grant-seeking that would try the skills of even a seasoned fundraiser. Mr. Landowne had some experience raising money as a volunteer but was not a professional. Ms. Newhouse confessed to never having raised a nickel in Jewish philanthropy and knowing nothing about the art of the ask. No matter; all of that would have to change, Mr. Fried and Mrs. Bernstein made clear. They intended to reduce their share of the *Tablet* budget within the next few years, so finding other major donors would be imperative. And the bulk of the burden would have to fall to Ms. Newhouse, despite her inexperience with foundations and her professed lack of skill.

"In most philanthropy, the person who is most directly responsible for the content, the creative core, the person who tells the story best, is the person people want to give money to and be involved with," Mr. Fried said, explaining why Ms. Newhouse needed to become the magazine's chief fundraiser. "People don't give money to the Metropolitan Museum of Art because they met the business manager. They want to talk to the director; they want to get to know the artistic vision behind the institution. At *Tablet*, that person is Alana."

Even for an experienced professional, the job would be far more difficult than a typical fundraising assignment for, say, a traditional charity or for a nonprofit institution in health or education or the arts. Not only was *Tablet* relatively new on the scene, and not only were its prospects limited to Jewish funders, but in the early 21st century, journalism was still a rare target for foundation dollars anywhere. (By the early 2020s, that was beginning to change, albeit very slowly.) Only a tiny number of foundations supported public-interest news media, and almost none of these had any particular interest in Jewish news. *Tablet* would thus have to make its pitch to an unprepared community of donors and foundations that had no experience in her field and were already fully committed to other, largely unrelated Jewish causes.

Ms. Newhouse did, as Mr. Fried noted, have some advantages in taking on this mission, though she was far from confident about them at the start. As befits an accomplished journalist, she is an excellent storyteller, eloquent in her command of *Tablet*'s vision and potential. She is charming and personable, although she acknowledges some impatience with uninformed opinions and irrelevant questions—a tendency that a good fundraiser would have to rein in. She also had the backing of two people who know the world of Jewish philanthropy better than practically anyone—Mrs. Bernstein and Mr. Fried—who pledged to add their influence whenever a prospect seemed promising.

Still, Ms. Newhouse recalls, "the process was so pressured. It felt so overwhelming. There was a sense of absolute urgency about it, and I was doing this on top of my regular job." The slow, gradual process of identifying possible donors, spending time with them, getting to know their interests and passions, inspiring them with a landscape of possibilities and opportunity, deepening their understanding of what makes the cause significant and timely—all of that takes persistence and patience. "And it didn't feel like we had time for that."

"When I first started," she elaborated, "sometime around 2014, I reached out to a friend of mine who does fundraising, and he said, 'OK, Alana, here's what you're going to do. You're going to have maybe 60 or 70 conversations. You're going to have to have multiple conversations with at least a dozen people, and maybe when you actually hit one who's a kindred spirit, at the third, fourth, fifth, maybe even seventh conversation, you'll get them.' And I looked at him and said, 'I don't have that kind of time.' But of course, in the end he was exactly right."

As Ms. Newhouse's friend would surely have predicted, the early results of her fundraising efforts were meager. In 2016, total donations outside of Keren Keshet amounted to $275,000, less than 7 percent of the budget, something Mr. Fried ruefully described as "a shrug of the shoulders." More months of effort followed, though even then—even with a well-honed, sustained pitch and a dozen or more conversations with seemingly kindred spirits—the earliest breakthroughs turned out to be dead ends in the long run. One series of meetings with a prominent real estate developer led all the way to a discussion about how he could help rethink and expand the print edition and how he might try to persuade two or three others to join him as major funders at the million-dollar level. But before long his interest waned, and the conversations ultimately went nowhere. Another prospect, a well-known attorney and investor, also came tantalizingly close but ended up the same way. Other appeals to boldface names in Jewish philanthropy reached the second or third conversation, but then the door closed.

One factor that made the appeal to big donors so complicated was the very thing that also made *Tablet* attractive to some prominent and wealthy people: It was becoming more and more widely known, more prestigious, and thus an attractive brand with which to be associated. It wasn't on a par with the Metropolitan Opera or the New York Public Library, to be sure, nor even the 92nd Street YMHA, but it was distinguished nonetheless, and influential. Still, that aura could easily give prospective donors the wrong idea: that sitting on the Board of *Tablet* might be a way of steering its coverage, of shaping what stories were written from what perspective for what kind of audience. For everyone at the helm of *Tablet*, including Mr. Fried, Mrs. Bernstein, Mr. Landowne, and Ms. Newhouse, that kind of interference in the magazine's journalistic independence was unthinkable. Nonetheless, it was hard to fortify those boundaries while also trying to entice and inspire people with a vision of being one of *Tablet*'s "owners."

In mid-2018, even as she was clarifying that Keren Keshet would soon reduce its support by 75 percent, down to $1 million a year, Mrs. Bernstein was nonetheless warning that the appeal to new funders needed to be unambiguous about maintaining journalistic integrity. Future donors need to understand from the outset, she urged Ms. Newhouse, that "*Tablet* continues on as it has been, and they will become investors in that magazine. I don't want to hear what they

Nonetheless, this was still not quite the solution that Keren Keshet had hoped for. Its goal had been to provide no more than $1 million a year or 25 percent of *Tablet*'s budget, whichever was less, beginning January 1, 2020. With expenses at Tablet running close to $4 million annually, that would have required recruiting three, not two, additional million-dollar donors. Unless a source could be found for the fourth million, only two other options remained: either reduce the budget to $3 million or increase the contribution of one or more donors.

Neither choice was viable. For starters, reducing the budget to $3 million would have caused Keren Keshet to cut its contribution to $750,000, if the foundation were to hold to its limit of providing no more than 25 percent. That, in turn, would have caused the other funders to make equal reductions, since they had promised only to match Keren Keshet dollar-for-dollar. The math dictated a downward spiral that would have killed the new funding partnership in its cradle and orphaned the magazine. But neither had any of the partners agreed to provide more than $1 million. So filling the gap with extra contributions was also, as matters stood, out of the question.

"Now it's a race to New Year's Day," Mr. Fried concluded at a 2019 board meeting, "to see if there can be another $1 million." The date was September 19.

The chances of finding another million dollars in 15 weeks were obviously close to nil. Rather than putting off an inevitable reckoning, the president of the Maimonides Fund, Marc Charendoff, made a final plea that ultimately opened the door to a solution. His foundation, Mr. Charendoff said, had always maintained a firm policy against ever making a grant solely so that some other funder could reduce its commitment. "We come in to be additive," he told the assembled board. But "after discussions with Arthur and Mem, we decided to do something we'd never done before, which was exactly that: to assume the funding that you had provided previously and not to be additive, which was a stretch for us and for our board."

He endorsed a continued effort to raise the needed funds, but in the meantime, "We all have to share the risk of ponying up a little more than we planned." He pointed out that Maimonides and Singer had already made other grants to *Tablet* for specific projects. Combined with some estimated earned revenue, this additional money would come to around $700,000. Counting that money, the total funding now on the table was $3.7 million—just $300,000 short of the goal. Rather than hold to a set of arbitrary rules that would destroy the very enterprise they were trying to save, he urged patience and confidence in an eventual success. "When you've gone from no revenue [beyond Keren Keshet] to $2 million of other revenue," he concluded, "it's certainly moving in a pretty impressive direction."

Mr. Fried and Mrs. Bernstein agreed to up their contribution by $300,000 to close the final gap, if that amount could not be raised by New Year's Day. The offer was made with the reluctant recognition that Keren Keshet's share of the budget would now be one-third, not 25 percent, and that it would be matching some commitments that were not unrestricted, like its own. Still, Mrs. Bernstein conceded, "In for a penny; in for a pound." Tablet would have what it needed to carry on for another year, while the fundraising continued.

———

More than a year later, as this is being written, the additional donation has not been raised. But *Tablet* carries on with the support of its three current backers. Some of the new board members have strained at the restrictions on interference in editorial decisions, though the rules have held so far, and *Tablet* continues to function as an independent source of news and commentary. "There have been moments of stress," Mrs. Bernstein acknowledged in 2021, "where some board members didn't like something that ran in *Tablet*. And they've struggled with that." She and Mr. Fried "try to step back and not interfere, but we make sure the board gives them total editorial freedom. And that seems to be working."

The coronavirus pandemic of 2020-21 put a temporary halt to the public events, but online readership and the audience for the podcast have remained strong. Additional podcasts have been added, too, including "Israel Story," about daily life in the Jewish state, "Anxiously," about ways of coping with various kinds of inner turmoil, and "Parsha in Progress," presenting differing perspectives on the weekly Torah passage. In August, the magazine began advertising for a marketing expert to take charge of promoting the podcasts and "grow our fan base."

More and more, *Tablet* is cited in mass-market newspapers and magazines for both its reporting and its commentary. Its politics are centrist but iconoclastic—inclined, as Ms. Newhouse has put it, to question "the interlocking infrastructure of elite institutions that made up American political and cultural life in the 20th century." It is, of course, staunchly pro-Israel, but with room for thoughtful critics of Israeli politics and government. It continues to straddle the boundary between upmarket, sophisticated writing for elites and puckish fun for just about anyone, including a casual readership.

Some of the material in the latter category—recipes, games, sports, trivia, and the like—can occasionally annoy Mrs. Bernstein (to her, a lot of it is *narishkeit*, Yiddish for frippery), but Mr. Fried considers it smart marketing and a good way to hold the interest of a diverse readership. In maintaining a mix of high- and lowbrow, the magazine has continued to honor a core tenet of the original Nextbook mission:

to open a wide portal onto the whole of Jewish life, a means of discovery and belonging that makes no demands but offers a banquet of ideas, information, observations—and, here and there, a bit of *narishkeit* for dessert.

"We are highly enthusiastic about it to this day," Mr. Fried said in 2021, in a long reflection on the history of Nextbook and *Tablet*. "Morty engaged a highly talented Jewish editor, and a creative person. She wanted to create fresh journalism, and that's what she got to do. Her creation. And we supported it, we continue to support it, because it's a great piece of Jewish journalism, and a gift to the Jewish people."

CHAPTER IV

ISRAEL

Nourishing Jewish Learning
in the Jewish State

At the time he and Mrs. Bernstein were envisioning Keren Keshet, Arthur Fried also held a seat on the board of Israel's Center for Educational Technology, known in Hebrew by the acronym MATACH. The organization works to improve teaching and learning in Israel and throughout the Jewish world—not solely with digital solutions, but through research, innovation, and creative programming of many kinds. Among several initiatives that combined digital and old-school learning methods, MATACH in the late 1990s was trying to instigate a widespread, dramatic upgrading of school libraries across Israel, both to bring them into the dawning digital age and to expand and improve their collections of physical books. To Mrs. Bernstein and Mr. Fried, who treasure books and believe in libraries as open temples of thinking and learning, the idea of enriching school libraries all over Israel had almost instant appeal. Being able to rely on the proven competence and creativity of MATACH made the idea all the more appealing.

It was, in some ways, a similar idea to the one that had motivated the American philanthropist and bibliophile Andrew Carnegie a hundred years earlier: A good library—well equipped, properly designed, and stocked with a rich collection of titles—was a model that, once perfected, could be replicated in many places, over and over again. If the recipients pledged to maintain the facility and its collection, a funder could supply all the physical requirements with a standard budget and workplan, then move on to other sites with essentially the same vision in mind. As Mr. Fried saw it, this was an ideal arrangement for a small foundation with a tiny staff, "because it does not require heavy programmatic overview and intervention and supervision and heartbreak. You know what you're doing; you know what you're spending on; you can watch it happen, and it does. And then you're done, and if you want to, you can then do it again."

So, among the first projects of what would become Keren Keshet—begun even before the foundation was incorporated under that name—was a series of library renovations and expansions that Mrs. Bernstein and Mr. Fried funded and carried out jointly with MATACH. Beginning in 1999 and continuing for another dozen years, in school after school the two institutions designed, built, and equipped new spaces for books, computers, and study areas, supported by nearly $9 million in aggregate grants. Even after the books were in place and the physical improvements finished, MATACH followed up with schools to help them use the equipment, develop programs for students, and generally ensure that the new libraries were well-maintained and well-used. As they had in the Jewish Community High School of the Bay, Mrs. Bernstein and Mr. Fried took personal care over the look and feel of these libraries—their design and atmospherics, the way they invited users in and encouraged them to explore, linger, and ponder.

One after another, Israeli schools began seeing little temples of reading and contemplation springing up in their midst. Because MATACH knew the educational landscape, had worked closely with the participating schools, and had proven it could deliver, the foundation could roll the idea out in multiple places without having to scrutinize separate budgets and workplans for each one. As Mrs. Bernstein put it, "We knew that if they got one right, they were going to get 20 right. The concept had already been perfected." And, she added, the opportunity to enrich the environment of so many schools in so many places had one additional benefit for the two trustees personally: "It was fun!"

Other foundation forays into Israeli education went far beyond improving libraries. Starting at the same time as the library project, Keren Keshet in 1999 made the first of what would eventually amount to $21 million in grants to design, build, and equip a new school, spanning kindergarten through 12th grade, that enrolls students from secular and devout families and every shade of belief in between. At the time the school was conceived, this was an exceedingly rare form of education in the Israeli state school system, which generally insists that parents choose between schools where religion is both taught and strictly observed and those where it is discussed (if at all) solely in cultural, historical, and social terms. This bifurcated system is a poor fit with a society in which, ample research shows, the great majority of families fall somewhere midway between the religious-secular polarities, neither strictly Orthodox nor un-religious, but broadly *masorti*—respectful of religious traditions and tenets and observant at least to some degree.

Before 1999, a very small number of Israeli state schools enrolled students on both religious and non-religious tracks, but these were generally in smaller or more remote communities that couldn't sustain two separate schools. In all of the country's large metropolitan school districts, the wall between religious and secular education held firm, regardless of the frustration of families torn between the two. One result was that students in the secular state schools might never meet their more religious peers, and vice-versa—a form of spiritual segregation that only reinforces needless societal divisions over faith and tradition.

In 1993, in a taxi ride with the then-mayor of Jerusalem, Ehud Olmert (later prime minister of Israel), Zalman Bernstein first heard of a young educator with a dream of bridging the gulf between religious and secular education. Ruti Lehavi, then 34 years old, had approached Mr. Olmert with a vision of a school she called Keshet (the name was unrelated to that of the foundation, which didn't yet exist). Her "rainbow" school would still offer religious education, prayer, and traditional observance for students who wanted them, and other forms of Jewish learning and tradition for the less- or non-observant. But it would otherwise teach all children together, essentially eliminating the barriers between them for most of the day.

Mr. Bernstein, enthralled, pledged the support of the AVI CHAI Foundation for the enormous challenge of planning the curriculum, staffing, and logistics of the new institution. Alongside the Jerusalem municipality, AVI CHAI paid for an expert team to create an educational blueprint of the new school from recruitment of students and faculty to teaching methods to the content of religious and non-religious Jewish Studies classes to forms of extracurricular activity. The foundation further helped in implementing the plan, with support for marketing, selection of faculty, curriculum development, and other essentials, including paying the salaries of some teachers not covered by standard municipal staffing rules. (One example: Every Jewish studies class at Keshet had two teachers, one avowedly religious and one not. For a time, the extra cost of the second teacher was borne by AVI CHAI.) The school opened, in premises provided by the municipality, in September 1995. Its faculty was distinguished, the class sizes small—rarely more than 20—and the curriculum was the work of some of Israel's best pedagogic minds. It became a signature AVI CHAI project.

The Keshet School's one great deficit was its campus. As the student body grew, grade by grade, it quickly filled an old and repurposed main building and gradually spread into a warren of caravans and other makeshift structures on a large public lot in Jerusalem's religiously and economically mixed Katamon neighborhood. The neighborhood's social mélange was ideal for a school that sought to unify families of different backgrounds, but the buildings and their surroundings gave exactly the wrong signal: Instead of showcasing a shining new approach to Israeli education, the structures gave the impression of an orphaned institution struggling in slum conditions. As Mrs. Bernstein succinctly put it, "The place was a dump."

Even if hadn't been so run down, the facility simply didn't have enough space. In the spring of 2000, as the school was completing its fifth year, Ms. Lehavi approached the foundation for an emergency grant of $200,000 to create four new classrooms. That would meet the immediate need, but she was adding a new class every year. Tacking on a few more classrooms was just postponing the real problem: The Keshet School was a success, and its site was too small to accommodate it. The foundation paid for the new classrooms but added another $100,000 to start planning a completely new campus.

As Mrs. Bernstein and Mr. Fried saw it, the essential last step in fulfilling the school's founding vision would be to provide a building as modern and distinctive as the education inside it. They persuaded Mayor Olmert to let them build on the opposite side of the public lot from where the current school stood—thus allowing the construction to proceed without interfering with regular school activity. In exchange, when the new school was complete, the foundation would clear away the old structures and provide the municipality with a first-rate playing field on the entire site, for public use as well as for the school.

To create the new building, the trustees turned to a known and respected architect, Arthur Spector, who had designed the headquarters of Yad Hanadiv years earlier, when Mr. Fried was taking the helm of that institution. He had also worked closely with Mr. Fried as the architect of Tel Aviv's Hemda Science Teaching Center, which Hanadiv had created and funded. Mr. Spector and his firm also designed an educational center for troubled teens, which was supported by Hanadiv, in the Lower Galilee. Among hundreds of the firm's projects both in and outside of Israel, these stand out in Mr. Spector's mind because of the close, detailed involvement of Mr. Fried and the foundations he piloted.

As a concept for the Keshet School building, Mr. Spector drew on his childhood memories of one-room schoolhouses in rural New England, some of which still existed near his family home when he was growing up in the mid-20th century. The small, single-room structures impressed him as intensely communal places where "everyone would study in that one room—five or six different levels of classes, no walls between them—where there was an enormous amount of interaction among students." The inclusiveness behind the idea of the Keshet School, the desire that students of very different backgrounds study and play and socialize in a single place, seemed to him like a grander version of those all-in-one American classrooms.

"That stayed with me as an image of how to bring people together," he said in a reflection nearly 20 years later. "So at Keshet, instead of just corridors and classrooms off the corridors, we brought everything together in the central part of the school, which is part of the entrance—a large open space which was, for me, like a one-room schoolhouse, except it was very large and encompasses the library, the beit midrash, the cafeteria, the teachers' rooms, and generally the public space of the school. It can hold more than 300 students for an event or graduation or a party or any kind of gathering."

A second story hovers above the expansive inner courtyard, overlooking the common area and contributing to a general atmosphere of "everyone together with no walls between them." From that central area flow two wings, one for the lower school and one for the high school, so that a child growing up in the Keshet environment would experience a physical continuity, from early childhood to late adolescence, that is nonetheless anchored on a common space where all ages interact.

Other spaces were designed to open up, allowing for larger groups to study together, including two mini-amphitheaters that could be used separately or for a combined, single class or gathering. Expansive windows, exterior balconies and courtyards, and areas for planting around the perimeter added to a feeling of inclusiveness in the building, where even the separation of indoors from outdoors was blurred.

Besides his architectural stature and his enthusiasm for the school's mission, Mr. Spector brought another advantage to the construction project: He and his firm were exceptionally well liked and respected at the Jerusalem Zoning Commission, where new projects can sometimes languish for years awaiting approval for changes in land use. Because the new building was going up on a site that had previously been open field, and plans called for reconfiguring the remainder of that field and the access routes into it, the project required a green light from the Zoning Commission—a fearsome prospect that could have forced most of the Keshet School's children to spend the rest of their education in dismal conditions. Mr. Fried and Mrs. Bernstein viewed Mr. Spector's rapport with the commissioners as an insurance policy against that kind of bureaucratic delay. And in the end, whether because of his influence, or that of the foundation, or that of the highly experienced and bureaucratically savvy project manager, Dan Wind, the project was approved in less than 18 months, an achievement that Mr. Spector still considers remarkable. Construction began in 2004 with an initial budget of $14 million, paid entirely by Keren Keshet. (High inflation in Israel's building industry in those years, plus some upgrades intentionally added during construction, raised the final budget by $7 million.)

As with the San Francisco high school, the libraries upgraded by MATACH, and many other building projects, the creation of the Keshet School was a project in which Mr. Fried and Mrs. Bernstein took a keen personal interest, and where their influence was extensive. Given Mr. Fried's long history of providing foundation support for building projects, both at Yad Hanadiv and AVI CHAI, he was accustomed to playing a lead role in site selection and keeping close watch on the design, permitting, and construction process, and especially on costs. He had clear ideas, rooted in experience, about how to strike the right balance between aesthetics and economics, producing high-quality, striking architecture within a reasonable (and closely monitored) budget. Here, too, Mr. Spector's long and successful association with Mr. Fried was an asset: He understood that the trustees would be a regular presence in the project's decision-making, and he valued their input. "It's a luxury," Mr. Spector said, "to have people holding the reins who are on top of every single decision and make decisions quickly and wisely. Arthur and Mem were outstanding—they listened to different ideas, were open-minded, but after a fairly concise process, they came to quick decisions. And that was essential for getting a quality building done quickly and on budget."

Sure enough, the new Keshet School was ready for occupancy in 2007, ahead of schedule and within the expected costs, and demolition of the old structures, followed by development of the expansive communal playing fields, started that same year. A community center on the property was likewise repaired and upgraded, creating an overall campus that was a first-rate community asset, educationally state-of-the-art, and aesthetically striking. It has contributed to the upscaling of the Katamon neighborhood's image, both by attracting families who want to enroll their children and by beautifying what had once been an eyesore.

As the school's reputation has risen, so has its enrollment and the diversity of its class offerings. The pressure from these forms of expansion has sometimes been unkind to Mr. Spector's initial vision for the building. In particular, some of his roomy, versatile open areas have been carved up or closed in to create more classrooms. "We have constant battles with people who want us to close off every possible courtyard and just add half a classroom here and a half a classroom there," he lamented.

But the need for additional learning space is beyond dispute—class sizes have increased by as much as 50 percent to accommodate higher enrollment—and opportunities to enlarge the building by adding a third story have so far not passed muster with the municipality. Though frustrated with the erosion of his design, Mr. Spector acknowledges the relentlessness of the pressure school leaders face: "It's almost impossible, because tomorrow morning's needs are obviously going to transcend any longer-term considerations. If they had twice the area, they'd still be missing two classrooms, always."

Growing pains, no matter how painful, are still the result of growth, and growth is usually the result of success. That has been the quarter-century-long story of the Keshet School. When Ruti Lehavi was preparing to open her first class, in 1995, she confessed that she had no idea how many families would be willing to entrust their children to a school that mixed religious, traditional, and secular students. Would she even attract enough takers to justify starting the first class? Twenty years later, with Keshet's own classrooms full beyond capacity, demand for similar schools was spreading across the country. The newspaper *Ha'aretz* reported in 2013 that "about 20 mixed schools now operate in Israel, from Shlomi in the north to Be'er Sheva in the south, along with a similar number of kindergartens. About ten additional schools are being established. But the big leap was the establishment of the Keshet School."[29]

As that leap recedes further and further into history, it has become hard for many Israelis to recall what was once so remarkable about it. And that is arguably the greatest sign of the school's success. In 2014, according to *The Jerusalem Post*, the chairman of the Knesset's Education, Culture, and Sport Committee visited one of the schools that follow the Keshet model. Watching the visitor and his entourage move from classroom to classroom, one student couldn't understand why a member of the Knesset would be going out of his way to visit a school.

"What's the big deal?" the student asked. Someone tried to explain that the chairman was interested in seeing a school where religious and secular students study side-by-side.

OK, the student asked again, baffled, "But what's the big deal?"[30]

Although Keren Keshet made dozens of contributions to improving K–12 education in Israel, amounting to some $35 million between 1999 and 2020, nearly 90 percent of that sum was devoted either to the Keshet School or to the MATACH library projects. Other contributions, though much smaller, went to influential programs that improved the teaching of particular subjects, including Jewish Studies, civics, history, or the science-math-engineering disciplines. A few grants went to individual schools, including two pioneering schools for religious girls: the Pelech School and the Tehillah School. But these came to roughly $200,000 each—tiny amounts compared with the Keshet School. Only one other K–12 grant in Israel exceeded $1 million, but it was a quintessential Keren Keshet venture: the renovation of Himmelfarb High School, a distinguished Modern Orthodox middle and high school for boys in Jerusalem's Bayit VeGan neighborhood.

Himmelfarb was far from a new institution in the mold of the Keshet School or the Jewish Community High School of the Bay. On the contrary, it was already a much sought-after destination for boys prepared to work hard to meet Himmelfarb's high standards and earn its respected diploma. By 2004, when Mrs. Bernstein and Evan Feinsilver visited the campus, Himmelfarb was several years into a modernization of its curriculum and teaching methods, under a relatively new director, Rabbi Jeremy Stavisky.

It helped that Rabbi Stavisky and Arthur Fried had known each other since childhood, having grown up in the same Brooklyn neighborhood. That fact reduced the need to conduct deep research into the principal's background before making a grant. But even without that advantage, Rabbi Stavisky had already made a name in Israel as a gifted educator, after several years leading and updating the school, and Himmelfarb itself was, as Mr. Fried put it, "long known as an outstanding school for religious Zionist boys, with a wonderful reputation." Backing the school was therefore a relatively easy decision for Keren Keshet.

At that point, Rabbi Stavisky was building a whole new reputation for Himmelfarb as a cutting-edge school for a new, 21st century market. He was also cultivating a religiously pluralistic environment, teaching a demanding curriculum of Modern Orthodox Jewish studies but providing a welcome for less religious and traditional students as well. Most important, he was establishing a culture of teaching and learning that emphasized wide-ranging inquiry, critical reasoning, an open exchange of ideas, and independent thinking. "Our students are taught that they have to understand the different worlds they live in, their intellectual roots, and the complex reality of being Orthodox Jews in a modern Israeli society," he wrote in 2004. "Students understand that we are trying to perform a complex theological and educational balancing act within a polarized society in which balance and compromise are out of vogue."[31]

A key quality that distinguished Himmelfarb in these years, Rabbi Stavisky wrote a few years later, was "its identity as *both* Orthodox and modern. As difficult as it is for these two attributes to co-exist in the United States, achieving their comfortable synthesis is that much harder in Jerusalem. Subjected to the powerful influence of fundamentalism, educators might almost be forgiven for advocating the less complex course of 'one truth' and disparaging the merit of modern Western culture. But we must have the capacity to acknowledge the inherent blessings of liberalism while, at the same time, continuing to uphold our values and principles as Orthodox Jews—particularly when the two come into conflict." Alongside the school's openness to the diversity of Jewish religious experience, it also sought to embrace the ethnic and economic diversity of Jewish Israel. "It is thus a privilege for Himmelfarb to serve a population that is not only half-Sephardic and half-Ashkenazi, but also 5 percent of which is of Ethiopian origin," he continued. "Some of our students come from families on welfare, while others come from affluent Jerusalem households."[32]

When the prospect of a Keren Keshet grant first arose in 2003, Arthur Fried's initial thoughts were that Himmelfarb was "led by a dynamic principal who has provided the school with the Zionist spirit, with fine education, and with a spirit of service. The school has a record of being the boy's high school in the country that has the largest number per-capita of graduates who continue in the Army for officers' training. It has a remarkable attitude in terms of social and religious values." It was exactly the kind of superlative Jewish education that he and Mrs. Bernstein consistently tried to support.

The physical premises, however, were anything but superlative. "Nothing is more dichotomous," Mr. Fried said at a 2004 foundation board meeting, "than an excellent educational institution that has done pioneering and groundbreaking educational work, housed in the most decrepit of circumstances." Mrs. Bernstein and Mr. Feinsilver had come away from their visit wondering how even the best teaching in the world could succeed in such surroundings. The 1960s construction was never beautiful—it was a characterless assembly of plain concrete boxes—but it had aged poorly over four decades, and Mrs. Bernstein was shocked to find broken doors, peeling paint, poor lighting, minimal and outdated equipment, and an overall musty, threadbare atmosphere that signaled little more than neglect and indifference. The school didn't need a new building, but it needed a new look and feel, including a completely new interior.

Rabbi Stavisky made no secret of his frustration with these grim surroundings, though he may not have been fully prepared for the foundation's nearly instantaneous response to his plea for help: "Jeremy called," Mr. Fried remembered, "and the answer was Yes. That's all. It was worthy." The foundation contacted architect Zvika Rubenstein who, in early 2004, began work on a plan for a completely new interior design. Among other things, Mr. Rubenstein's firm was the creative force behind much of Jerusalem's sprawling Shaare Zedek medical complex, including its master plan. Keren Keshet had been supporting the hospital since 2001 and knew his work well.

The transformation of Himmelfarb was swift and sweeping. In went fresh lighting and air conditioning, including a new building-wide electrical system, plus bright colors, better windows and doors, truckloads of new fixtures, modern labs, a fully redesigned library, and other up-to-date educational spaces. As in their other school projects, Mrs. Bernstein and Mr. Fried were determined to wrap a quality education in an uplifting and invigorating physical package, where students could experience, both practically and subliminally, the importance and excitement of what they were doing. Although the boxy exterior could not be altered much, the interior became modern, bright, well-equipped, and flexible—an ambience of excellence for an excellent education.

"It was Keren Keshet's privilege," Mr. Fried concluded in a 2020 interview, "to support Jeremy's work at the Himmelfarb School. He is a great educator who makes a great impression on his students. He asked for our help, and he deserved it, and we were pleased to give it."

———

Measured solely in shekels or dollars, Keren Keshet's support for formal education dwarfed every other category of its grantmaking in

Israel. But in some ways, the foundation's support for cultural organizations and events was arguably more far-reaching and significant. With a total of roughly $14 million between 1999 and 2020—barely more than one-third of its outlays on education—Keshet grants poured life into more than 60 Israeli cultural projects, from music to literature to the graphic arts. Even when the individual grant amounts were small by the foundation's standards, they were often major donations in the context of the chronically undercapitalized arts sector. And in a few cases, the grant amounts were remarkable by any measure and contributed to significant growth and enrichment in Israel's cultural landscape.

Keren Keshet's transformative support for Hebrew Book Week in Jerusalem is the clearest (and, in financial terms, the largest) example. Because the international market for books in Hebrew is relatively small, Israeli publishers rely heavily on domestic sales, and thus on the enthusiasm of the Israeli public for both new and classic titles. The Hebrew Publishers Association has for many years hosted an annual festival for its members to present their wares, though for many of those years it was a drab affair—usually just long rows of tables with piles of books on them, perhaps a sign overhead bearing the publisher's name or logo. The only activity available for visitors was the obvious one: going from table to table looking at books. Jerusalem has plenty of book lovers, and the event was amply stocked with titles new and old, so it drew a regular crowd of people who were already looking to buy. That was apparently all that many vendors wanted. Like most trade groups, the Hebrew Publishers Association had only a modest budget, and its leading members didn't see much advantage to spending more than the minimum on an annual sales event.

But when Evan Feinsilver visited Hebrew Book Week in 2000, in Safra Square adjoining City Hall, he found it shockingly dull and dispiriting. He soon learned that Mrs. Bernstein and Mr. Fried had long shared his frustration and believed that a great opportunity was being missed here. As the two trustees saw it, this was not just an unimaginative business decision by the publishers, it was a disservice to Hebrew literature. What the booksellers regarded as a sales event Keren Keshet saw as something that could be much bigger: a cultural celebration, an opportunity to engage families and introduce children to the joy of reading, a forum to showcase great Israeli writers, and a spark to kindle pride in the beauty of the national language. Surely, they reasoned, there were ways a foundation could inject some joy, color, and fun into the event while simultaneously boosting the publishers' prime objective of selling books.

At the trustees' request, Mr. Feinsilver turned to Tsila Hayun, a gifted events coordinator then in her early 40s, whose firm, called Hotam, devoted much of its effort to deepening the public's understanding of Jewish and Israeli culture. Among many other projects, Hotam organized a reading-encouragement program for children in libraries, funded by the Jerusalem Foundation, and the Autosefer, a mobile bookshop with reading programs for children, which Keren Keshet sponsored for three years. From the perspective of mission, business, and style, Ms. Hayun—a devotee of culture, manager of a successful enterprise, lover of books and libraries, and master of sparkle and creativity—was a near-perfect fit for Keren Keshet. Mr. Fried and Mrs. Bernstein asked her to submit a proposal for livening up the coming year's book festival, and she leapt at the chance.

"I asked them, 'What's the budget?'" Ms. Hayun told *Hadassah Magazine* a few years later. "They said, 'There isn't one.' So I wrote the proposal as if it were an exercise where I had an unlimited budget and could wish for anything I dreamed of. I made a plan where books were the attraction. Not food, not TV stars. We'd have book events all over the place. We started with Jerusalem. I said, 'Let's go for the whole city.' It was just what they wanted."[33]

Her first-year budget ended up rising above $300,000—hardly exorbitant on the scale of major American cultural events, but close to unprecedented for a literary festival in Israel, especially considering that it covered only the "extras," not the core functions of bookselling. Still, the "extras" were extraordinary, as Mr. Feinsilver remembers them. When the next Hebrew Book Week opened the following June, he said, "It was like a bombshell. She completely transformed the square with lighting and banners and decoration, and she hired a video company to project text and images onto the walls of the surrounding buildings. Next to the square is a garden, where she made a children's area with a stage and performers and authors reading books and interacting with the children."

And when Ms. Hayun said, "Let's go for the whole city," she meant it literally. She sent writers and books to more than a dozen cafés and community venues all over Jerusalem, so that those not tempted to venture down to City Hall would nonetheless have a piece of Hebrew Book Week in their own neighborhoods. Rami Mishan, owner of the upscale Café Masaryk on trendy Emek Refaim, was surprised when Ms. Hayun asked if she could hold a literary event in his restaurant in 2001, but like many other restaurateurs in the city, he gave it a try. "It had never been done before," he told a reporter five years later, "but it sounded like a good idea. The first writer we had was Eyal Megged," a celebrated American-Israeli poet and novelist. "It was very successful, so we kept doing it. Now everybody does it, and the line to get in runs into the street."[34]

In Safra Square, Ms. Hayun ran a near-continuous sequence of public programs featuring authors, books, and films, complete with a full-color program booklet giving schedules and profiles of the participating authors and artists. Weeks of newspaper ads and media outreach created a public-relations crescendo leading up to the festival. The public response was so

overwhelming that the following year, Keren Keshet agreed to nearly double the budget so similar events could be mounted in Tel Aviv and Be'er Sheva. The sheer exuberance of the now-national festival was unlike anything in Israel's cultural history.

It was an expensive undertaking, however, costing Keren Keshet close to two-thirds of a million dollars every year. And for all their popularity with the public, the cultural extras that the foundation and Ms. Hayun brought to Hebrew Book Week were never much of a hit with the publishers' association. The group was, and remains, a trade association for an assortment of businesses struggling to prosper in an increasingly difficult market for printed books. It is not a cultural organization, and its mission is not, in Ms. Hayun's phrase, "socially conscious." As a result, the association and the foundation never forged a shared vision for the event, and when Keren Keshet sought to reduce its contributions, neither the association nor anyone else was willing to shoulder the responsibility for continuing most of the enhancements it had made.

The foundation continued supporting Hebrew Book Week for six years, with its final grant in 2007, just as the international financial crisis was taking a toll on the Keshet endowment. Some aspects of Ms. Hayun's "bombshell" have survived—even today, the event is livelier and more festive than in the past, which is surely attributable at least in part to the Keren Keshet investment. But some of the luster has been lost, and the more spectacular and costly aspects of Ms. Hayun's plan have ceased.

Other cultural grants in Israel were more modest, both in budget and ambition, but they may have had longer-lasting effects. For example, a decade of support for a musical event at the annual Israel Festival in Jerusalem made it possible for more than 5,000 people a year to hear outstanding Israeli music at only a nominal ticket price. The festival is a prestigious showcase for the arts, both from Israel and abroad, spanning several weeks in the spring, but its events can be expensive to attend. Keren Keshet's support, totaling more than $1.5 million over roughly a decade, brought at least one part of the festival well within the means of most Israeli families. By the time its grants ended in 2013, many more of the festival's events were offering subsidized admission.

Separately, a nearly 20-year stream of grants to the Zamir Choral Foundation, totaling more than half a million dollars, contributed to the growth of an extraordinary network of youth choirs, now in 13 U.S. states and eight localities in Israel, performing great Jewish choral works.[35] A 2018 survey of alumni and current singers found that participation in HaZamir not only honed young people's musical skills, but more to the point, deeply strengthened their Jewish identity, their attachment to the state of Israel, and their sense of unity with Jews who are different from themselves.[36] Participation in HaZamir has risen and spread over the years, not primarily because of Keren Keshet's support, but certainly with the additional fuel its grants provided.

Unlike the much larger grants for Hebrew Book Week, these were not meant as transformative investments. They were responsive, additive grants that bolstered, in significant ways, good work that was already under way and that showed promise of going further. Support for dozens of other cultural organizations and programs was similar: sustenance or added fuel for work of already-demonstrated quality. Without attempting to change or create anything new, these grants enriched beloved assets of Israeli culture and, in some cases, like that of HaZamir, helped strengthen cultural bonds between Israel and the Diaspora.

Still, Keren Keshet's intervention in Hebrew Book Week was remarkable for the scale of its vision. In that way, it was typical of many of the foundation's largest and most significant initiatives elsewhere: It sought to elevate, invigorate, and enrich an important element of Jewish life that had the potential to gather Jews of many backgrounds around their common heritage. The point of the Hebrew Book Week investment was not necessarily to erect a permanent structure of activities that would continue intact and indefinitely. It was to demonstrate the value—cultural, social, and economic—of an invigorated festival of literature, and then let the market and heightened popular demand dictate what form that would take.

At least to some extent, that goal was achieved. The festival, Mr. Fried noted in 2020, "was there before we came and is still there after. It gets broad support from the publishers, from the Jerusalem Foundation, from others. And the improvements that we made, many of them, continue beyond us."

The third largest category of Keren Keshet's grants in Israel was dedicated to supporting the country's civic life—its national coherence, its fidelity to its founding principles, the effectiveness of its democratic government, and the future of its leadership. In all, the foundation devoted some $9 million to this broad field, much of it for research, conferences, and policy development aimed at nurturing a democratic society aware of its past and prepared for the future. Among the largest of these grants was more than $1 million for the construction of the Menachem Begin Heritage Center, which houses the former prime minister's papers alongside conferences and public programs centering on Mr. Begin's vision and legacy.

Nearly $2 million in total was devoted to research, conferences, and publications in half a dozen prominent forums. One was a quarterly series of symposia on constitutional government, held at Tel Aviv University, that gathered experts from Israel and the United States on "the theory and practice of liberal democracy," which the foundation sponsored from 2002 to 2009.[37] Another, also at Tel Aviv University, was the Chaim Weizmann Institute for the Study of Zionism and Israel, which hosts multidisciplinary research into the meaning of Zionism, past and present, and which includes a Young Scholars Forum for doctoral and post-doctoral students.[38] Grants to the Metzilah Center for Zionist, Jewish, Liberal, and Humanist Thought underwrote years of research and policy analysis "integrating Zionism, Jewish values, and human rights in the Jewish State."[39] Foundation grants beginning in 2017 helped establish Pnima Israel, a new research and advocacy institute created "to address the rifts and polarization in Israeli society."[40] In 2017, the foundation gave half a million dollars to Shalem College, one of Zalman Bernstein's signature ventures, to help it establish Shalem Press, publishing classics of Western democratic thought in Hebrew translations, as well as works of Jewish political theory in English. And nearly a dozen years' worth of grants sustained a Post-Holocaust and Anti-Semitism Project at the Jerusalem Center for Public Affairs, a research center specializing in public diplomacy and foreign policy.

But alongside these more cerebral pursuits was a nearly 20-year-long stream of grants, amounting to considerably more money than went to any of the think tanks, devoted to nurturing the soul and vision of future leaders. The grantee, Beit Prat Israeli Midrasha, operates a network of study centers where some of the cream of Israel's Jewish youth immerse themselves in Judaism's core texts and classics of the Western canon and explore the implications for their futures and that of the country. Beit Prat brings young people together for four months in 25 cohorts across Israel, studying subjects ranging from Bible and Talmud to Hebrew Poetry to Jewish Thought to Yoga. The goal is not solely intellectual learning, but a cultivation of "meaning, community and purpose."[41] A late-summer program enrolls some 200 participants a year from across the religious spectrum, from strictly observant to purely secular, for 40 days of study on a similar range of topics.

With more than 3,000 alumni at the time this is written, Beit Prat has set itself no less a goal than creating "a new Israeli mainstream" that transcends and repairs the cultural and religious fissures among the country's ethnic, ideological, spiritual, and geographic communities. The program's alumni go on to cultivate social and learning networks of their own, advancing the ideas and sense of community forged in Beit Prat programs and continuing the fellowship that began there. When the Covid-19 pandemic brought much of Israel's social and academic worlds to a standstill, Beit Prat seized the opportunity to upgrade its technology and expand its roster of activities online. These included not only virtual versions of its regular programming for young people, but a new series of online programs for Israeli leaders, including senior politicians and security officials, business executives and entrepreneurs, and influential journalists.

The founder and director of Beit Prat is Micah Goodman, a celebrated author and lecturer known throughout Israel as an inspirational voice for Israeli Jewish unity and identity. He is also Arthur Fried's son-in-law—a fact that meant the program was already deeply familiar to the Keren Keshet trustees, but that also required some extra effort at objectivity in assessing its potential. Beit Prat's rising popularity in Israel's young leadership circles provided much of the rationale for the foundation's support, irrespective of family ties: Even during the worst of the pandemic in 2020, when the program's signature gatherings and study sessions could not be held in person, enrollment reached a new record. "They have four times as many applicants as they have spaces," Mr. Fried pointed out, "and they charge money to attend. This is something you really have to want to do. And people want it."

Apart from the large investments in think tanks and Beit Prat, Keren Keshet made dozens of smaller contributions to basic elements of Israel's quality of life, including community-based mediation programs, the Association for Public Health Services, and the Center for Green Living in Jerusalem. Separately, many small grants for projects in Jerusalem flowed through a specially tailored organization, the Devorah Foundation, which Zalman Bernstein created in the late 1990s. Keren Keshet made annual contributions to Devorah of roughly $1 million each for the better part of a decade, through 2008, and then gradually wound down the project with a few years of declining support thereafter.

"Devorah" had several meanings, beginning with the obvious reference to the Biblical judge and prophetess (Judges:4-5). But the word also means "bee" in Hebrew, and the bee was a symbol dear to Mr. Bernstein, one he incorporated into his company's original logo. The new charity, bearing this subtle but very personal reference to its prime donor, was an outgrowth of Mr. Bernstein's close friendship with Ehud Olmert, who in 1993 became Jerusalem's first Likud mayor. The previous mayor, the Labor politician Teddy Kollek, had created the Jerusalem Foundation as a vehicle for private donations to city-sponsored projects that could not be funded fully from government budgets. But Mr. Olmert, from the opposing party, soon found the Jerusalem Foundation less responsive to his priorities, so Mr. Bernstein offered to set up a new vehicle to back municipal initiatives of the new regime. Thus began what ultimately totaled $11.5 million in mostly small grants for civic-improvement projects around Jerusalem.

At first, the grants were just a scatterplot of minor initiatives with no strategic pattern or unifying purpose. Each year, municipal departments were invited to submit ideas to Devorah, with the understanding that no department would receive more than $150,000. In practice, most departments submitted many projects totaling much more than that maximum, so after Mr. Bernstein's passing, Mr. Fried and Mrs. Bernstein would choose among them to keep the total outlay to $1 million or $1.5 million, depending on the year. The results were usually nice enough—a renovated gym here, a community garden there, a one-off cultural event somewhere else—but with little effect on the city's overall quality of life. Worse, because the proposals came from every branch and discipline of local government, and were spread over Jerusalem's entire 48 square miles, it was nearly impossible for the foundation to keep track of how the money was used and whether the results really merited the amounts spent on them. It was, in essence, an annual gift to the municipality with few strings attached.

After a few years of this, Mrs. Bernstein and Mr. Fried pulled in the reins and increasingly concentrated Devorah's donations on renovating municipal kindergarten playgrounds. They retained a single architect who could acquire material in bulk, replicate successful work in multiple places, and make widespread improvements that benefited tens of thousands of children. In some ways, the idea followed the same pattern as Keren Keshet had established with MATACH in school libraries: develop a successful model, then stamp it out in place after place. The idea was naturally unpopular with much of the city bureaucracy, since it primarily enriched the Education Department to the exclusion of many others. But as a method of philanthropy, it was eminently more sensible—and probably more effective—than sprinkling small amounts across the entirety of the municipal landscape.

As mayors came and went (Mr. Olmert left office in 2003, and two successors followed in the next half-dozen years), the relationship between Devorah and the municipality grew more distant. When Keren Keshet's assets took a hit in the financial crisis of 2008, and Mr. Fried and Mrs. Bernstein started looking for less-essential branches of work they could trim, it became clear that Devorah's time had come. Beginning in 2009, projects that had already been approved were gradually completed, but no new ones were entertained.

Still, Evan Feinsilver argues that the years of small projects, even if not particularly exciting as expressions of creative philanthropy, had real accomplishments that directly enriched communities all over the city. "It was a way to contribute to Jerusalem," he points out, "and to do many good things that weren't big enough or prominent enough to get money in other ways. And they did make a real difference to people, with projects for children with special needs, for neighborhoods, for sports, for things that improve people's lives."

———

In fact, well beyond Devorah's micro-level grantmaking, Keren Keshet's work in Israel has fueled scores of other projects with relatively small amounts of money, contributing to schools and parks, festivals and scholarships, synagogues and community centers, programs for youth and for the elderly and for everyone in between. More than 100 Israeli organizations and projects each received $50,000 or less over the foundation's first 20 years.

Asked to name some of the projects she found the most satisfying, foundation director Linda Sakacs chose one of these small grantees in particular: Beit Issie Shapiro, Israel's leading provider of services, therapies, and advocacy for people with disabilities. Founded by a pioneering philanthropist who devoted nearly all his charitable wealth to the cause of eliminating the barriers posed by disability, Beit Issie Shapiro is barely 40 years old and still regards itself as a "social start-up." It was not a Keren Keshet initiative, and all the support it has received from the foundation has come in four- or five-figure annual contributions. But it is the kind of results-driven organization in which Zalman Bernstein might have discerned a "royal reach." In 2011 it won Israel's "Most Effective Nonprofit" award and has since earned other Israeli and international recognitions for innovation and impact.

Beit Issie Shapiro falls outside any conceivable diagram of Keren Keshet's core interests in Israel. A foundation that primarily trains its resources on Jewish learning and literacy, on culture and identity, and on the durability and cohesion of the Jewish State might not seem a logical source of money for an organization focused on disability. And it's true, Keren Keshet did not commit large sums in this case—its total contribution to Beit Issie Shapiro over 20 years was a little more than $125,000. Nor did the foundation make any special demands about how the money would be used. But the donations were that most precious and scarce kind of support for any nonprofit: largely unrestricted, to be spent on whatever the grantee most needed.

"For a foundation with so little staff," Mrs. Bernstein said, in a reflection on the role of such small, unrestricted grants, "we want to support as many good organizations as we can, but we can't research and monitor them all. So when we find great leaders, people who

deliver, we respond to that. We back winners. And we fund organizations that are run by those people, doing quality work with real impact, where we don't have to worry about what they spend the money
on. We see the results, and we know the leaders. And when we can,
we help them."

CHAPTER V

THE FORMER SOVIET UNION

Securing a Jewish Future

Since at least the late 1990s, a foray into post-Soviet Jewish life had become a prime ambition of the AVI CHAI Foundation, and Mrs. Bernstein and Mr. Fried were determined that the newly formed Keren Keshet would play a role in making that expansion possible. Ultimately, their goal would be to establish a sophisticated grantmaking program for AVI CHAI, based in Russia and extending at least to Ukraine. That program would need an experienced staff member based in Moscow and at least one AVI CHAI Trustee with firsthand knowledge of the Russian Jewish community. But to get there, the two trustees believed it would first be necessary for Keren Keshet—with its wider latitude for experimentation, its greater tolerance for philanthropic risk, and its ability to consult privately and informally with other donors—to clear a path for AVI CHAI to enter and set up shop. They quickly focused on at least two distinguished operators in Russia (with others soon to follow) who could serve as Sherpas on their journey into Jewish philanthropy in the former Soviet Union.

The first of these was George Rohr, founder and chief executive of NCH Capital, a private equity firm with extensive holdings across Eastern Europe and the former Soviet Union. Mr. Rohr offered not only intimate knowledge of Russia's business, cultural, and political environment, but just as important, broad and deep experience as a Jewish philanthropist there. Alongside generous financial support for Chabad programs at universities and in Jewish communities across Russia, he had created the Rohr Jewish Learning Institute, a source of curricula and educational programs in several languages, eventually including Russian, operated by Chabad.

"For many years, he was a lay leader of the beginner's service at the great synagogue Congregation Kehilath Jeshurun," Mr. Fried observed several years later. "He was a most distinguished philanthropist, a teacher, and a wise businessman, one of the first Westerners to invest in the former Soviet Union and make money there. George knew his way around. He was intelligent, experienced, Jewishly committed. He had everything AVI CHAI needed."

The foundation's second high-level guide into post-Soviet Jewish philanthropy was Russia's young, dynamic chief rabbi, Berel Lazar, who had been a leader in Chabad's rapid expansion across the former Soviet Union in the late 20th century. Rabbi Lazar was not only revered in Jewish circles but highly respected and well-connected in the secular sphere as well. Among many national honors, he was awarded Russia's Order of Friendship in 2004 and the Peter the Great First Class Order in 2005, both in recognition of his contributions to interethnic and interreligious understanding and harmony. As a founder of the Federation of Jewish Communities of the CIS (the Commonwealth of Independent States, composed of most of the former Soviet republics), he stood at the center of Jewish communal and philanthropic life across the whole of the post-Soviet world.

The co-founder of the Federation of Jewish Communities, alongside Rabbi Lazar, was another eminent Jewish businessman and philanthropist in Russia, Lev Leviev, who soon became a partner to Keren Keshet. Mr. Leviev's Ohr Avner Foundation, established in 1992, supports a wide network of Jewish educational institutions in the former Soviet Union. The son of a rabbi and a self-made billionaire, Mr. Leviev was born in what was then the Uzbek republic of the USSR and made Aliyah with his family, arriving in Israel essentially penniless at age 15. There he took a job in a diamond polishing plant, and after a stint in the Israel Defense Forces, he started his own diamond polishing business. After moving to Russia, he expanded first his diamond enterprise then his portfolio of other investments, which included real estate and chemical companies. From what became an enormous fortune, he founded Ohr Avner and became an indispensable ally and funder of Chabad.

The head of Ohr Avner, Rabbi David Mondshine, completed the list of advisers and partners that Mrs. Bernstein and Mr. Fried assembled, during frequent visits to Moscow, to help them design their charitable program for the former Soviet Union. As Mr. Leviev's chief philanthropic operative, Rabbi Mondshine offered something essential that Keren Keshet was unable to supply on its own: frontline executive leadership with the ability to get things done in an environment that, to Western eyes, was sometimes inscrutable and rife with opportunities for missteps. With introductions orchestrated partly by Mr. Rohr, in 2000 Mrs. Bernstein and Mrs. Fried began learning, especially from Rabbi Lazar, what needs Keren Keshet could fill.

———

As in nearly all its other work, the foundation sought projects that could be time-limited, rather than launching an indefinite stream of grants on which organizations would forever depend for their survival. In other parts of the world, that goal wasn't always achieved as intended—foundation support for the Jewish Community High School continued for much longer than expected, for example, and *Tablet* continues to rely on annual grants from Keren Keshet. But in Russia, there was no room for error. With no local staff to be their eyes and ears, Mr. Fried and Mrs. Bernstein were especially loath to create long-term dependencies 5,000 miles from their door. Instead, they hoped for projects on which they could provide startup capital, reasonably confident that local philanthropy, perhaps rallied by Mr. Leviev and Chabad, would then cover the grantees' ongoing costs.

Rabbi Lazar had a couple of initial projects in mind. One was the establishment of internet cafés in four localities with large Jewish populations and limited Internet access. Because so much of Chabad's offerings—as well as other Jewish cultural and educational resources—are available online, opening the Internet to more Jewish families seemed like a timely, relatively quick undertaking that neatly fit Keren Keshet's preferred model. Its support, which eventually totaled just over $1.5 million, could create the cafés and provide seed capital to start operations, after which they would be self-sustaining.

The second initiative was also a tech venture: the creation of a website (eventually named Jewish.ru) that grew to resemble a Russian version of *Tablet*: a compendium of Jewish news and cultural coverage, with a smattering of lighter fare on sports, food, and prominent personalities. Although Keren Keshet's $70,000 contribution to Jewish.ru was much smaller than for the cafés—which have become less necessary as broadband has grown more widely available—the website has continued and thrived. Two decades after it was established, Jewish.ru still prominently displays special thanks on its front page to the Rohr Family Foundation and Keren Keshet. (AVI CHAI later created a more specifically literary web magazine in Russian, also modeled on *Tablet*, called Booknik.ru, which likewise continues to this day.)

But these were small, introductory gestures, nowhere near the scale at which the foundation planned to invest. A third idea, only slightly larger than the first two, was the creation of all-purpose Jewish community centers in four major cities of western and central Russia: Nizhny Novgorod, Ufa, Yekaterinburg, and Novosibirsk. The centers comprised the essentials of Orthodox Jewish life, including a synagogue, mikvah, clinic, library, and space for children's programs and other communal events. Keren Keshet committed $2 million to their construction, with the understanding that community donations and philanthropy would cover the ongoing operating costs.

A year later, an idea for a much larger and more personally rewarding project emerged in a conversation in Moscow between Mrs. Bernstein and Rabbi Lazar, based on an anecdote she remembered hearing from Mr. Fried. In the mid-19th century, Mr. Fried had told her, Adèle de Rothschild had established an orphanage, mostly for Jewish children, in the rue Lamblardie in Paris's 12th arrondissement. The institution was founded at a time when the number of Jewish orphans in Paris was outstripping the number of Jewish families able to take them in. It provided not only care and shelter, but education and traditional Jewish observance, along with a job training program for the boys. It helped ensure that children with no family would grow up healthy, Jewish, and well equipped for independent life. Perhaps, Mrs. Bernstein suggested, something similar would be useful in Russia?

Useful indeed. Rabbi Lazar described, for example, an ad-hoc orphanage in Moscow that was essentially a private home, where the resident couple had taken in homeless Jewish children one by one, in increasing numbers, until there was no more room for anyone. Homeless children in Russia, he explained, are normally cared for in state-run institutions, where religion and ethnicity are not part of the program, and children normally grow up with little sense of their individual roots or culture. Some of these institutions are poorly run or understaffed, so the overall level of care is often less than ideal. But even in the best cases, a child would be unlikely to emerge with any knowledge of Judaism or Jewish identity. A properly equipped, well-staffed Jewish orphanage would be a blessing to the community as well as to the children who stayed there. But it would be a substantial capital project, costing millions of dollars to build and even more to operate.

Intrigued but cautious, Mrs. Bernstein next took up the idea with Mr. Leviev, who endorsed the plan almost immediately. He asked Rabbi Mondshine, on behalf of Ohr Avner, to draw up a plan for financing, construction, and operations. In May 2005, he formally proposed a partnership with Keren Keshet to build two residential facilities for about 70 youngsters each, one in Moscow and the other in Zhytomyr, Ukraine. A month later, after vetting the proposal with Yehuda Cohen, director of a highly regarded children's home in Israel, the foundation responded with a commitment of up to $5 million. A portion of the grant could be used for operating expenses for the first four years, but by the end of that time, local contributors and Ohr Avner were expected to assemble enough money to cover the ongoing costs. Ohr Avner would cover all educational expenses from the outset.

Although the financial arrangements were negotiated without much difficulty, it wasn't long before correspondence between Ohr Avner and Keren Keshet raised a completely unexpected question about operations: What criteria would determine which children were eligible to be admitted?

Mrs. Bernstein and Mr. Fried had presumed that orphanages were for orphans—children with no living parent or guardian. That would have seemed to be a fairly objective qualification for admission, requiring little further elaboration, but the reality was not so simple. "Orphanage," they learned, was just an imprecise shorthand; in Russia, as in some other places including Israel, group homes for children serve multiple functions, including congregate foster care, protective services, and state custody. Children in these facilities would not, in fact, all be without living parents. Some may have been abandoned; some might have parents who are incarcerated; others may have been taken into custody for their protection or may have been surrendered by parents who are unable to care for them.

The trustees found the news jarring at first, given the substantial money they had committed under a basic misapprehension. But Mr. Cohen—whose own organization, Beit Elazraki Children's Home in Netanya, also hosts children with a mix of difficult backgrounds—assured them that the situation was both normal and desirable. Residential care, he pointed out, was no less urgent for many children suffering from neglect, abuse, abandonment, or extreme poverty than for those with no parents. With that understanding, Mr. Fried and Mrs. Bernstein readily agreed that the most important target for admission to the new group homes should be Jewish children, orphans or not, who are already living in state-run institutions. But beyond that, they reasoned, local Jewish leaders would be the best judges of any further criteria, and the matter was left to their discretion.

Construction proceeded on the community centers and the two children's homes over the next several months, by which time Rabbi Mondshine and Yehuda Novick, Keren Keshet's chief financial officer, had established a close working relationship. Given the challenges of monitoring a project from 5,000 miles away, the foundation was largely relying on Rabbi Mondshine for reports on the progress of construction and on how the money was being used. That required some dialogue, however, as Mr. Novick explained some years later: "In Russia, organizations aren't used to reporting to foundations from outside. Here, they worked closely with Lev Leviev and Ohr Avner, and anything the funder asked for, they would supply. It was totally open, but it was kind of ad-hoc. They weren't used to drawing up formal budgets, submitting progress reports, and so on. But now here comes another organization, and we're asking for a lot of detailed records to substantiate the things we were spending money on. For example, I asked them for documentation on the purchase of the parcel in Ukraine—which I had to put in Google Translate because of course it was all in Russian—just to do some basic due diligence. They were happy to send it to me, but they weren't used to that."

At the same time, Mr. Fried and Mrs. Bernstein also brokered a relationship between the Federation of Jewish Communities of the CIS and Yehuda Cohen, the Israeli children's home director and expert on care for troubled youth. Mr. Cohen's program at Beit Elazraki is an international model of congregate care that is the opposite of institutional—rich with arts and physical activities, religion, counseling, and family-style meal and social time. With Mr. Cohen's guidance, the Federation gradually re-imagined the kind of care and services it intended to provide, expanding from a simple combination of dormitory and school into something richer that more closely resembled family life. One small but telling example: The children all slept on trundle beds, which could be opened to accommodate a friend for a sleep-over. Other children could invite friends to spend the night, the Federation reasoned; why should these children be different?

For Keren Keshet, this expansive and compassionate approach to

residential care was a mixed blessing—the enriched services and programs added to the operating budget, which the foundation was un-
derwriting, but it was a profound improvement in the children's lives.
With Rabbi Lazar's oversight and Mr. Cohen's professional consulting and example*, the new model created the kind of comprehensive
Jewish environment that few Russian families—and certainly no
state-run orphanages—could have provided. Both Keren Keshet and
Mr. Leviev considered the benefits well worth the extra cost. To be
sure, those costs would eventually have to be borne by local contributors and philanthropists, but by then, the funders believed, their benefits would be evident and donations from the community would be
easier to raise. The backing of international donors, wrapped in the
combined prestige of the United States and Israel, would also make
a favorable impression on those who wanted to be sure they were supporting a quality, sustainable venture.

By early 2006, Rabbi Mondshine was reporting that one of the orphanages, the one in Zhytomyr, was nearing completion and about
to be partially occupied, and all but one of the community centers
were now built and open. The remaining projects, the orphanage in
Moscow and a community center in Ufa, were under construction and
were expected to open within a year. Still, although Mrs. Bernstein
and Mr. Fried made frequent visits, the 5,000 miles separating Keren
Keshet and Ohr Avner were hardly ideal for the normal due diligence
expected of an organization investing more than $10 million in a
faraway set of real estate developments. Despite having full confi-

---

* Mr. Cohen's organization, Beit Elzraki, received a $10,000 foundation grant in 2006 in
thanks for his role in the project.

dence in the openness and honesty of Rabbi Mondshine, his foundation, and the Chabad network that operated the centers and orphanages, Mr. Novick believed it was important for him and director Linda Sakacs to see the work firsthand. Mr. Fried and Mrs. Bernstein agreed, and the two officers set out in the summer to visit the unfinished projects in Moscow and Ufa and to see the newly operational children's home in Ukraine.

The trip left a deep impression on them both, not only for the encouraging progress on construction and operations—which were exactly as Rabbi Mondshine and his colleagues had reported—but for the obvious need the centers and homes were filling in thousands of Jewish families, in what had for decades been a wasteland of Jewish religious and communal life.

Visiting the home of the newly installed rabbi in Ufa, where a new community center was under construction, Mr. Novick remembers asking the rebbetzin where the nearest mikvah was. She answered that she had to fly to Moscow every month, or else drive to another city 11 hours away. Mr. Novick remembers thinking that, under those circumstances, it was all but impossible for most Jewish families in Ufa—home to perhaps as many as 10,000 Jews[42]—to observe the laws of *taharat hamishpachah*, or family purity. Earlier that day, in his visit to the construction site, Mr. Novick had gotten to know the contractor building the community center, where a new mikvah was to be one of the last parts of the finished building. But that phase wasn't scheduled to be finished for nearly another two years. After hearing of the hardships of the rebbetzin and other religious women in Ufa, Mr. Novick negotiated a change in the construction schedule. A new mikvah was completed in a few months.

But what Ms. Sakacs and Mr. Novick experienced in Zhytomyr, where the new orphanage was partly completed and occupied, was a degree of need far more profound and urgent. There, the two foundation officers met the first 12 abandoned, orphaned, or neglected children experiencing, often for the first time, a supportive family-like environment surrounded by caring adults and an embracing affirmation of their Jewish heritage. They also met other children who would eventually benefit from the part of the new facility that was still under construction.

In Moscow, where the facility was not yet occupied, they accompanied a social worker to the home of one family whose children might be eligible for admission. It was instantly clear that the children's mother was struggling with mental illness and, despite obvious intelligence, she seemed wholly overwhelmed with the responsibility of raising the children, whom she was trying to home-school. As a result of a chaotic home environment, the children were behind in their education and suffering from emotional and physical problems. One child appeared to be on the autism spectrum; he plainly needed specialized education but wasn't receiving it. In encounters like this, Mr. Novick wrote in a report to the foundation trustees, "it was difficult to hold back the tears."

The Moscow home proved more difficult to complete than the one in Ukraine, largely because of complications with permitting and licensing as applications ground through the Russian bureaucracy. The project dragged along for another three years before opening with nearly 80 young residents in 2010. But within just a few years, the two institutions managed not only to establish a model for modern, compassionate, and thoroughly Jewish residential care for children, but fueled a Chabad program that grew, by 2016, to encompass four residential and educational complexes in Russia and Ukraine. Together they housed a total of 350 children, with plans for more.[43] In 2019, less than a decade after the Moscow home opened, Rabbi Lazar installed the mezuzah on a new expansion wing that doubled the building's capacity.[44]

"A year after we ended in Russia," Mr. Fried recalled more than a decade later, "we went back and asked Rabbi Lazar, 'Did we do good?' And he was overwhelmed by the question. That made us feel terrific."

Testimony to the good work of Keren Keshet in the former Soviet Union came not only from the elders but from the children as well. Mrs. Bernstein was particularly touched by a thank-you gift from the residents of the Zhytomyr home: a set of tiny candlesticks the children had made themselves. She promised that she would use them to light Shabbat candles in her home in Jerusalem, which she continues to do to this day. Perhaps, she added, "you may someday be there too." She adds with pride: "Some of them are, in fact, in Israel now that they're grown."

"It worked out very well for us," Mr. Fried concluded. "Both social welfare and religious growth. The things we started continued, and many of the children have gone on to lead successful Jewish lives. Quite a happy ending."

CHAPTER VI

NORTH AMERICA

Prayer, Learning, and Good Works

By the early years of the 21st century, Lincoln Square Synagogue, where Zalman Bernstein's Jewish journey began, was practically bursting its travertine walls. The burgeoning congregation had for years been cramped in the shul's distinctively rounded sanctuary, and the constant, intensive use of the facility was accelerating the need for costly structural repairs and modernization.

Indeed, by some measures, the building had never been big enough. Former congregation president Morton Landowne marveled in 2013 that the City of New York and its Fire Department had ever allowed the building to be occupied. "From the moment of its first use," he wrote in *Jewish Week*, "it was clear that the lobby space was far too small, and its entrance and egress routes were dangerously inadequate. The sanctuary itself, despite the egalitarian beauty of its circular shape and banked pews, was forbidding for those disabled by illness or old age."[45] By 2005, both physically and economically, the building had reached a breaking point.

In 2006, Rabbi Shaul Robinson, who had succeeded Shlomo Riskin and Saul Berman as the synagogue's senior rabbi, and the board of the congregation negotiated a real-estate swap with American Continental Properties, which owned a large parcel less than half a block away. In exchange for vacating the old synagogue at 200 Amsterdam Avenue, moving to 180 Amsterdam, and surrendering the air rights over its new building, the congregation would receive nearly $20 million from American Continental. That was expected to supply two-thirds of the money needed to build a modern, much larger shul on the new site.

Rabbi Robinson and the board then formed committees to raise the remaining $10 million and to oversee construction. The mission was to create a striking new building worthy of what had become one of America's most important and influential Modern Orthodox congregations. Among the first prospective donors they contacted was Keren Keshet, which promptly pledged $1 million, paid out over three years from 2007 through 2009. Other contributors, large and small, made up nearly all the remainder, including some of the synagogue's least wealthy members, each of whom had been asked for a donation personally by the senior rabbi.

But despite the fundraising success, it wasn't long before the construction plans started to unravel. By the time Keren Keshet's last payment was made, unbeknown to the foundation, the prospects of ever completing the building were looking doubtful. Within a year, "doubtful" would become "improbable," as construction flaws mounted, costs soared, and lawsuits volleyed back and forth. On October 11, 2010, the project ground to a halt, out of money and mired in conflicts among contractors. Some prominent members, *The Forward* reported, feared that this moment "marked the beginning of the end for the storied synagogue."[46] One member of the board recalls taking his family on a round of visits to other Manhattan synagogues, sadly contemplating the day when they would no longer have a spiritual home on Amsterdam Avenue.

The root of the crisis lay in the very things that had made the project inspiring to so many donors: the grandness of its vision and the devotion of the people behind it. The committee originally formed to oversee construction focused most of their attention on creating a stunning piece of architecture, retaining the award-winning global design firm CetraRuddy with instructions to create a monumental place of worship—but setting only the vaguest limits on the budget. To save the substantial cost of hiring a project manager, the committee sought to oversee the project itself, despite having no members with experience on big construction projects. At least one major contractor turned in seriously defective work, and some others performed less than ideally. CetraRuddy, for its part, rose to the challenge of designing an awe-inspiring building, but with some features that, a later review would conclude, were far beyond the synagogue's means.

Rabbi Robinson and his board, confronted with the unfolding disaster, took two immediate steps. First, they quietly began to formulate a Plan B to save Lincoln Square, including the possibility of selling the property back to American Continental and renting more modest quarters somewhere nearby. Second, they disbanded the original committee and replaced it with one that was heavier on relevant expertise, including finance, construction, and management. They asked the new panel to assess the situation, to determine if the project could still have a future, and if so, to estimate what it would cost to restart construction and finish the job.

The committee immediately launched an exhaustive round of interviews with every participating firm, starting with the architects and builder and proceeding through all the subcontractors, in an attempt to understand exactly what had happened and what it would take to right the ship. "I don't think anyone understood how bad it was until we got deeper into it," a member of the new committee recalled several years later. "I was prepared to jump ship, because I thought we were in for a catastrophic collision. In my heart, I felt we were at a dead end, facing a vast, vast gap." Still, they forced themselves to retain some vestige of hope, evaluating candidates for construction supervisor and possible replacements for defective contractors, in case the project could somehow be revived.

The overriding problem, of course, would be the budget. The project had burned through nearly all the available money, and it was barely 60 percent done. As the committee drew closer to a full understanding of what had been accomplished and what remained to be completed, it learned that just remediating defective work already performed would cost at least $1 million, probably more. The newly poured foundation was fatally flawed; fire marshals determined that the building's power supply was insufficient; the sewer connection had to be re-dug; the roof on an adjoining building would have to be reinforced. The problems with past work kept mounting even as the estimates for finishing the remainder of the building steadily inched upward. As the new cost estimates mounted, the committee member said, "we went from a problem to a big problem to what seemed like an insurmountable problem."

Based on their initial survey and analysis, the committee members told Rabbi Robinson that the only way the new synagogue could be built is if he raised at least another $20 million. It seemed to them, at that point, all but impossible. Every likely source of major donations had already been tapped, often for large sums. And who would give more to an organization that had already spent close to $30 million only to land in so much trouble?

What they did not yet know was that Rabbi Robinson had turned in desperation to Mrs. Bernstein and Mr. Fried, frankly disclosing all that had gone wrong and asking if they could help him close the gap. To his amazement and relief, they quickly responded with a letter on November 4—less than four weeks after construction had been halted—agreeing to consider a $20 million donation if their concerns and questions could be confidently resolved. The concerns naturally included wanting to know, as Mr. Fried later put it, if "this is actually the right number. How can we be sure, if they ran into trouble before, that they won't find themselves with cost overruns again?"

To help answer those questions, Rabbi Robinson carefully disclosed to the committee that a ray of hope had emerged, if they could furnish a solid number and defend it. Without naming names—in fact, only on condition that he *not* disclose a name—he explained that a possible donor would consider giving nearly the entire amount needed, provided that the prospects of completing the work on budget were clear and convincing.

But at that point, the committee's inquiries were still underway. The estimate of $20 million was the best one available, and the promise of a new development team—including the strongest of the original contractors, plus some key substitutions and the addition of an expert project manager—would considerably improve the odds of success. None of this amounted to a guarantee, nor would it yet have been possible to furnish one. But it was based on the kind of diligence and experienced judgment that had been lacking in the project up to that point.

Steven Spira, a retired business executive who had run his own manufacturing company for many years, served as the committee's "numbers person" in a meeting with Mr. Fried and Mrs. Bernstein in early 2011. The two trustees' questions were, as expected, pointed, and Mr. Spira's answers were frank—confident where he had solid knowledge, cautious where he didn't. He noted that CetraRuddy had pared back the more prohibitively expensive elements of the design without losing its elegance. The builder and project manager were outstanding. The numbers were the result of the development team's expertise and the committee's meticulous review.

At the end of the discussion, Mr. Fried and Mrs. Bernstein stepped out of the room and, reading her old friend's apparent sympathy for the project, Mrs. Bernstein suggested, "Let's just tell them we'll do it." "No," Mr. Fried countered, "let's wait to put it in writing, so there are no misunderstandings." She agreed, and when the two re-entered the room, they appeared sympathetic but noncommittal. Mr. Spira went home that night with more hope than he had felt since beginning the project, but he was still doubtful that his mission had been accomplished.

"When the rabbi called me two days later," he remembers, "and asked me to come to the synagogue, he showed me the e-mail. I was flabbergasted. The two of us had a drink together. Mem and Arthur had kept their cards close to their vests, so it came as a total shock to me. The amount they gave was beyond anything we could have imagined. It felt miraculous."

The congregation was informed that their synagogue would be built after all; the "insurmountable problem" had been surmounted. Almost no one, however, was told who the surprise donors were. The final condition of Keren Keshet's extraordinary donation was that the source of the money not be identified. ("We didn't want to be the address for every synagogue in trouble," Mr. Fried explained later.

"This was Mr. Bernstein's shul. His Jewish growth had roots in that institution. It was unique. We weren't in the floundering synagogues business.")*

Unfortunately, as often happens in troubled real estate ventures, Mr. Spira's confident numbers became less confident over time. Within a year, as experience overtook projections and theories, the costs again began to escalate—but this time, not by nearly as much as before. A lawsuit left over from the earlier construction period went against the synagogue; installation of the signature 5,000-square-foot glass façade cost more than even the maximum the glaziers had estimated; the heavy front doors proved more complicated than expected to hang. Although the list of surprises was long, each of them had a feasible solution. Still, the solutions would add to the cost, and the synagogue would once again be in the position of having to find millions of dollars—upwards of $3 million—with all its likely sources already fully tapped. There was only one place to turn.

"I'd like to believe that our sincerity was helpful," Mr. Spira suggested, looking back roughly a decade later. "We gave them honest numbers and explained when we were wrong. But I didn't pledge my firstborn. Rabbi Robinson didn't give them a brilliant sermon. In the end, I think it was Zalman Bernstein and his legacy, and his relationship to the synagogue, that made it happen."

That much was true. "It was Zalman's synagogue," Mrs. Bernstein later confirmed, "and a lot of the things he did, his largesse, his kindness, a lot of his philanthropy, came from there. So they needed a little more, and we gave it."

---

* As time passed, the trustees eased this restriction, and today a plaque honors Keren Keshet's role in rescuing and completing the new building. It is one of very few such public recognitions of the foundation anywhere in the world.

Still, although Lincoln Square was at the core of Zalman Bernstein's spiritual and philanthropic life, the grant bore little relation to his style of philanthropy. His aversion to philanthropic bailouts was so adamant that he had it inscribed into the mission statement of AVI CHAI: *"The foundation will not fund deficits."* He preferred to back unambiguous successes, not to mitigate failure. A project six years behind schedule and at least 70 percent over budget would not likely have piqued his enthusiasm.

"He would never have made that grant," Mr. Fried concluded. "Never. This was not a Zalman grant. It was Mem Bernstein and Arthur Fried, period."

What led them to make such an extraordinary gift, more than any connection to Mr. Bernstein's life story, was that Lincoln Square was unique. Not merely a large and vibrant congregation, Lincoln Square was a launchpad of Modern Orthodoxy and an exemplar of effective Jewish outreach, which has drawn generations of younger Jews to a more observant, devoted Jewish life. As Morty Landowne wrote in his *Jewish Week* reflection on the synagogue:

What Rabbi Shlomo Riskin and the LSS founders created in the early 1960s was nothing less than American Judaism's model synagogue. Rabbi Riskin fashioned one imaginative program after another, and together they became the standard by which any aspirational congregation, of any denomination, must measure itself: Does it reach out to the community beyond its four walls? Does it concern itself with social and political action? Does it provide adult education? Is everyone made to feel welcome? Is the State of Israel a palpable concern of its congregants? None of those things could be taken for granted in the typical synagogue of 1965.

And what of its neighborhood? . . . LSS and its programs were the spark that illuminated the entire West Side and made it the pre-eminently vital Jewish community in America, and a model of what a Jewish community can be—must be—if it is to remain relevant and thrive.[47]

There was another reason for the Lincoln Square grant, which had to do less with the synagogue's universal significance and more with its significance to Mrs. Bernstein personally. Her circle of close Jewish friends lived mostly on Manhattan's West Side, and many were avid members of Lincoln Square. It was the spiritual capital of her community in New York, and she knew firsthand what a crushing loss it would be to hundreds of congregants if the synagogue went under. Although Mr. Fried was wary of becoming the favored philanthropic address of "every synagogue in trouble," Mrs. Bernstein knew that he would support this particular bailout. "Arthur did this mostly for me," she acknowledged. "That's how we operated. We looked out for each other, and when something meant a lot to one of us, the other did everything to support it."

For all the tumult and drama behind the building's financing and construction (a final budget shortfall in 2012 drew yet another $1 million from Keren Keshet, this time in the form of a loan, now fully repaid) the new Lincoln Square Synagogue manages to live up to its storied past and its place in the vanguard of American Judaism. The 52,000 square-foot building—the largest new synagogue in New York City in more than 50 years—became an instant landmark, winning multiple architectural honors.

Its undulating façade consists of five ribbons of glass in the form of unfurled scrolls, lined with brass-colored fabric simulating parchment, to represent the five books of the Torah. A spiral interior walkway symbolizes, as CetraRuddy's website puts it, "the infinite and continual study" the Torah inspires[48]. The horseshoe-shaped sanctuary, carried over from the original synagogue's design, is canopied in the ceiling's 613 lights, which correspond to the number of the Torah's commandments. The feeling of cosmic radiance they evoke won a 2016 International Lighting Design Award. ("If the Starship Enterprise had an Orthodox synagogue," congregation president Richard Kestenbaum told *Jewish Week* in 2013, "this is what it would look like."[49])

The Torah scrolls were transferred from the old synagogue to the new one on January 13, 2013. Although the congregation is smaller than at its peak in the 1980s, when Mr. Bernstein first attended, that is largely because Lincoln Square has inspired many imitators and is no longer the only dynamic Modern Orthodox congregation in New York. Its many religious and cultural programs, its continuing outreach efforts, its popular services, even its celebrated dining facilities all speak to a continuing place among America's best-known and most creative synagogues.

Change, of course, is constant. "For the Jewish community," Rabbi Robinson told *The New York Times*, "nothing in our experience is truly permanent, even a synagogue. This is a chapter, as opposed to a final destination. Jews are always on the march."[50]

Meanwhile, "It's a beautiful place," Mr. Fried observed in 2020, when the new building was approaching its eighth birthday. Both the structure and the activity it encompasses, he concluded, make it "a shining light on Amsterdam Avenue." The light nearly went out, but not quite.

"God protects communities when they try to glorify His name in the world," Mr. Spira said. "God also protects people who are foolish. So we qualified on both counts. We'd been foolish, but we also accomplished something that will glorify God."

For Keren Keshet, the extraordinary support for Lincoln Square was an outlier, given both the huge sums involved and the dire condition of the grantee. True, many other foundation grants also went to synagogues—in the United States and Israel, in the former Soviet Union, even a congregation in Australia—but all of these combined did not approach the amount of money devoted to Lincoln Square. In general, grants to synagogues, largely to support the growth of Modern Orthodoxy, were a steady but small portion of Keren Keshet's total philanthropy.

A far larger part of the foundation's giving was in the form of gifts to enrich Jewish education. Including big-ticket grantees like the Jewish Community High School of the Bay, the Keshet School, and the Himmelfarb School, along with the schools participating in MA-TACH's library program in Israel, support for schools amounted to a great deal more than was devoted to houses of worship. Many of these also bore the hallmarks of Mr. Fried's and Mrs. Bernstein's personal engagement in how projects were conceived and how the money was used. However, several others—like a $1.8 million grant toward creating a new campus for the Abraham Joseph Heschel School on Manhattan's Upper West Side, or a $3 million stream of grants to the elite Ramaz school on the Upper East Side—entailed no direct involvement by the trustees. In these cases, the foundation simply contributed toward the schools' ongoing needs, confident that they had already proven their excellence and their ability to use the money wisely.

But as in Israel, grants to advance Jewish education in North America weren't limited to schools. One of Keren Keshet's most original education projects helped launch a web-animation program originally called G-dcast (a play on "podcast"), in which teams of illustrators, animators, writers, musicians, and scholars produced cartoon videos illustrating portions of the Bible, and later parts of the Talmud and other aspects of Jewish life and tradition.

The project was the brainchild of Sarah Lefton, a digital media producer who conceived it as a response to wide gaps in her own Jewish education. A rising new-media star in the Bay Area, Ms. Lefton came to the attention of Mem Bernstein just as she was beginning to experiment with animated interpretations of the weekly Torah portion. At Mrs. Bernstein's initiative, a $50,000 Keren Keshet grant in 2008 helped produce some of the early G-dcast videos, and $123,000 more the following year helped Ms. Lefton and her teams put dozens of new ones online. She eventually produced at least one episode for every weekly Torah portion. For major holidays, other videos dramatized the relevant Bible stories; videos on the Psalms and Proverbs introduced visual and musical interpretations of Biblical poetry.

Each production was the work of a different team, featuring different styles of animation and narration—sometimes straightforward storytelling, sometimes a blend of drama and exegesis, and sometimes pure song. For example, in a video on *Megilath Ruth*, singer-songwriter Alicia Jo Rabins sings the convert's inner thoughts while a gentle animation enacts the key events of the story, beginning with Ruth's widowhood and ending with Naomi's embrace of the infant Obed. A recurring chorus of Ms. Rabins's song contains a version of the Book's most famous lines: "Where you go, I'll go; where you live will be my home; I will walk with you until the day I die." Toward the end, at Obed's birth, the lyrics hint at the great lineage to come: "Generations pass; generations come; and now our separate histories are one."

At the end of the video's final credits, the last screen reads, "Made possible by a generous gift from an anonymous donor." Keren Keshet, as usual, had asked not to be named.

The project, later renamed BimBam, won another foundation grant in 2015 to help it branch out from dramatizing Bible passages to a more challenging series on Talmud. The result was a reverently whimsical treatment of some famously dense material. In "Talmud Tales: The Rise of Yavneh," for example, the beginning of the story of Tisha B'Av starts at a party in a vaguely classical setting, but where the music and the characters' demeanor—and in some cases their clothing—suggest something more like a frat house. Addressing one another as "dude" and "bro," in dialogue peppered with "awesome," "chill out," and "cool," they nonetheless faithfully act out the story of Bar Kamtza's treachery and the subsequent ethical and religious arguments among the rabbis.

Some of the story's more famous passages are rendered faithfully, in an ever-so-slightly solemn tone that alerts the viewer that here is a significant statement to be pondered. The animated figure of Rabbi Zechariah ben Avkulas, for example, poses the critical question, "Is he who blemishes [a consecrated animal] to be put to death?" The text is directly from the source, and he speaks it before fatefully recommending that his brethren do nothing ("Hey, what's the worst that could happen?"), thus haplessly inviting the fury of the Roman empire and the destruction of the Second Temple. The moment carries much of the weight of a classic text, but with cheerful anachronisms that lower the psychological barriers for young people and invite them to reckon for themselves the complex questions of religion and realpolitik.

These subtle balances of playfulness and gravitas become evident only with multiple viewings. They otherwise flow by almost seamlessly, and not by accident. Each video was the product of a multidisciplinary team assembled by Ms. Lefton precisely to manage this blend of lightness and weight, anachronism and historicity. The stories and interpretations were under the guidance of Zvi Septimus, a Talmud scholar who later went on to the University of Toronto, Harvard, and Yale, who helped the teams of artists visualize the texts without distorting them. "I explained to them that their job is not to say what the story means," he told a reporter for *Tablet* in 2013. "Their job is to reproduce the rich ambiguities of the original."

Still, the videos were obviously not meant to be a scholarly resource or a forum for theological debate, and they don't attempt to capture the Talmud's full density and complexity. Shai Secunda, a Talmudist at the Hebrew University and editor of the Talmud Blog, told *Tablet* that he feared that the whimsy and drama of the series could be misleading. "The vast majority of the Talmud is intricate legal and theological discussions," he said. "These films are telling the sexiest, most modern and postmodern stories we have, but it's not what most of the Talmud is." Even so, he noted, "It might be useful for bringing people into the Talmud."

That indeed was the point. BimBam, like so much else that Zalman Bernstein and his executors funded, was at heart an exercise in outreach: a way to bring in Jews like Sarah Lefton, whose Jewish education was spotty but who were drawn to learn more, understand more deeply, and find paths of exploration that might lead them further into knowledge, faith, and practice. For them, as well as for teachers who use the videos in their classrooms or parents who might watch them with their children, each of the entries is accompanied by a downloadable source sheet and other notes to help a viewer delve deeper.

Sadly, BimBam reached a funding cliff in 2019, when Ms. Lefton could no longer raise the sums she needed to continue producing at the program's accustomed level of quality. By then, the organization had posted more than 400 original videos. They had drawn 11 million views and were distributed, along with the source sheets and notes, to at least 5,000 Jewish educators.[51] Fortunately, none of this creative output was lost. The Union of Reform Judaism agreed to host the entire collection as part of its website, where it is still available under its original domain name, BimBam.com. Consequently, Keren Keshet's quarter-million-dollar investment not only helped launch an 11-year endeavor that informed and inspired thousands of viewers, but it contributed to a permanent body of groundbreaking work that continues its mission of education and outreach, long after Ms. Lefton and her colleagues moved on to other work.

"It wasn't a large amount of money," Mrs. Bernstein observed a year after BimBam closed, "but it was a great project—original, creative, and just beautifully done."

———

Though most foundation projects in North America were aimed at advancing Judaism and drawing Jews more deeply into Jewish life, a few had simpler, more traditionally charitable goals: easing the burdens of life for Jews in difficult circumstances like poverty, illness, or disability. This was not a line of grantmaking that Mr. Fried or Mrs. Bernstein pursued in any systematic way. Rather, they responded to people they encountered who embodied *chesed* and showed skill and ingenuity in doing good. Then, when they could, they helped to expand or continue that work.

A noteworthy example in Brooklyn, on East 14th Street in the Midwood neighborhood, is something that, to all appearances, seems to be a clothing shop called "Bobbie's Place." In fact, the appearances are mostly correct—the store offers children's clothing attractively arranged with fitting rooms and mirrors, with a check-out counter for the final selections. Except for one anomaly: The clothes are free. The shop serves a neighborhood full of large families, many of them struggling on small incomes. The clothing is donated or purchased with donated money, but consistently high-quality, in conservative styles appropriate for a mostly Orthodox community.

It began in in 1988, soon after the passing of Renee Schick, matriarch of a distinguished Brooklyn family of learned, enterprising children and grandchildren. She had been the proprietor of Schick's Bakery, a popular gathering spot for the sprawling Jewish community in and around Borough Park that she founded as a young widow in 1943.* Besides being a revered local figure in her own right, she was the mother of Marvin Schick, a Jewish educator and legal scholar who had been an adviser and friend to Zalman Bernstein and Arthur Fried. (He continued as a consultant to AVI CHAI until his death in 2020 at age 85.) When Mrs. Schick's grandchildren set out to memorialize her with a clothing program that would honor both her entrepreneurial skill and her kindness, Mr. Bernstein and Mr. Fried each offered them personal donations of $18,000 as challenge grants to help raise the money they needed. Bobbie's Place (a variation on "bubbe," for "grandma") was thus born in a Brooklyn basement, tended by a granddaughter with nothing for furnishings but large plastic bins full of used clothing.

Over the course of more than two decades, the small charity has grown into a model of social enterprise, with operations in five cities,

---

* Still in business and since renamed Schick's Gourmet Bakery, it is widely regarded as one of the finest bakeries in New York, particularly renowned for its macaroons and Eastern European delicacies.

distributing brand new clothes to more than 9,000 children every year.[52] Along the way, Keren Keshet made nearly annual contributions from 1999 through 2012. By that point, the support totaled nearly three-quarters of a million dollars, including a $300,000 interest-free loan in 2004 to help pay for a significant expansion of the premises and the creation of the upscale-looking boutique that it has since become. One year after making the loan, Keren Keshet forgave nearly all of it.

"Bobbie's place started with two $18,000 gifts," Mr. Fried recalled with pride, "and turned into a most remarkable organization, which Keren Keshet had the honor of supporting over the years. We gave them operating support; we gave them capital. And what they have done with it has been truly impressive."

Another long series of grants also underwrote humanitarian work to ease the suffering of people in distress, in this case hospital patients and their loved ones. Between 2003 and 2018, the foundation gave a total of $1.5 million to a visiting chaplain program founded and led by Rabbi Simeon Schreiber, which started in the New York metro area and then moved primarily to South Florida. The program was widely recognized as a model of spiritual care for those in physical or emotional pain, based on Rabbi Schreiber's decades of experience consoling the isolated elderly, ill and recovering patients, and the family members who suffer with them and, in the worst cases, endure the grief of losing a parent or child.

One grant supported a project especially close to Rabbi Schreiber's heart: the creation and operation of the Bikur Cholim Suite at Mount Sinai Medical Center, where families of patients could sleep overnight on Shabbat in order to spend the day with an ailing relative. Although it was just one initiative among many, it was typical of

Rabbi Schreiber's approach to his mission. No one, he asserted in promoting the project, should have to spend Shabbat alone without a loved one, especially in a time of hardship.

What distinguished his program, in the minds of Mrs. Bernstein and Mr. Fried, was not that it would necessarily transform the field of chaplaincy services nationwide or reinvent the concept of spiritual care for the sick and dying—though it may have helped raise the standard of practice in the field by its example. What made the program a worthy grantee, in their eyes, was simply that it was excellent, in both its human and administrative aspects, and that Rabbi Schreiber represented the best of Jewish spiritual care in some of the most difficult circumstances. The foundation continued to back him until his death, at age 80, in 2018.

"He was simply the right man in the right place at the right time," Mrs. Bernstein said shortly after Rabbi Schreiber's passing. "He felt a calling, and he answered it. And we were there to help him."

CHAPTER VII

CONCLUSION

'Our Own Sense of
What We Wanted to Do'

In December 2013, Arthur Fried inserted into the minutes of the year's final trustee meeting a reflection on Keren Keshet's first 14 years of grantmaking, describing a drama unfolding in three acts. In the earliest years, he wrote,

> the foundation funded or acquired real property for philanthropic purposes which changed, to some degree, the nature of the foundation's balance sheet from solely cash and securities to include real property as well. It was also a period of significant philanthropic spending that enabled the creation of two anchor projects—JCHS and Nextbook—along with very substantial institutional support for a number of important projects for the benefit of the Jewish community in North America, Israel, and the [former Soviet Union]. . . . Since that period, approximately 50 percent of the corpus was spent or, sadly, destroyed in the market meltdown of 2008. . . .

Since 2008, the Foundation has continued to support anchor projects and maintain regular involvement with them, paying close attention to their continued development while, at the same time, carefully reducing support for them, given the Foundation's new financial circumstances. . . . Keren Keshet's finances were further impacted by a grant of 10 percent of its capital to the satisfactory completion of the new Lincoln Square Synagogue (a house of worship where the Foundation's benefactor returned to his Jewish roots, motivating his stupendous philanthropic benefaction for Jewish charity).

Keren Keshet is now entering, and the trustees have been working toward, a more circumspect philanthropic program so as to husband the Foundation's assets whilst remaining faithful to its philanthropic responsibilities and IRS distribution requirements. During the next four years, the trustees, with the help of decent financial markets, hope to regain some portion of what has been distributed, one might say, successfully, during the past five years. The trustees will be dedicated to those goals, and, to achieve them, will require much care and discipline, both in portfolio management and financial and philanthropic oversight and administration.

The financial catastrophe of 2008 left a trail of scorched earth across much of American philanthropy, seriously depleting the wealth of many foundations and sharply curtailing support for the charitable sector for several years. For Keren Keshet, however, it brought about not so much a crisis as an opportunity for recalibration, a rethinking of the foundation's scope of grantmaking and its ambitions for the future. Even in the second period, as the Great Recession was abating post-2008, Mr. Fried and Mrs. Bernstein resolved to maintain, monitor, and only gradually wind down their investments in the big projects that had dominated the early years. Thanks to a combination of strong financial management and a disciplined oversight of their biggest philanthropic projects, they were able to prepare their major grantees for eventual reductions in support without abruptly pulling the rug from under them. Even in these years of restraint, they could make a giant new commitment to Lincoln Square Synagogue without much hesitation.

The "more circumspect philanthropic program" that began in 2014 entailed a slight diminution in the number and variety of commitments, along with the cessation of some multiyear grant streams that the trustees regarded as having run their course. But even this more restrained regimen still allowed considerable latitude for seizing opportunity, backing enterprising leaders, and experimenting with new ideas. Even as total outlays declined by as much as 20 percent by 2016, Keren Keshet was able to make major new commitments to Chabad of San Francisco, the B'nai B'rith Youth Organization, a new Israeli think tank called Pnima, Jerusalem's Pelech High School for Girls, and *Tablet*'s experiment with a print edition, among other ventures.

Even in these years of retrenchment, the style and spirit of Keren Keshet's philanthropy remained essentially the same: a joyful, unbureaucratic extension of support—"with warm hands," in Mr. Fried's words—to effective organizations and creative people, cultivating religious and charitable assets across the Jewish landscape. Mrs. Bernstein's and Mr. Fried's decision not to operate a standard "strategic" foundation, with established programs and predetermined goals, staffed by subject experts and governed by long-term plans, gave them the freedom to exercise a more fundamental, exuberant kind of philanthropy. Theirs was a form of mostly unpremeditated giving—apart from a few large initiatives designed to build institutions over many years—that allowed money to flow to projects simply because, as Mrs. Bernstein put it, "they were good, and we saw potential in them."

––––––––––

In his now-classic survey of U.S. philanthropy, *The Foundation: A Great American Secret,* Duke University scholar Joel Fleishman distinguishes between what he calls "instrumental giving," in which donations are aimed at tackling and solving some societal problem, and "expressive giving," in which donors "show support for a cause or organization . . . larger than themselves," without concern for whether their grants fundamentally alter the world.[53] Both kinds of generosity, in Professor Fleishman's view, are necessary and valuable. However, "for most foundations, instrumental giving is the more appropriate and effective focus—much closer to the foundation's mission."

Under Mrs. Bernstein and Mr. Fried, Keren Keshet pursued both kinds of philanthropy, but most grants were supportive in nature, fortifying or expanding good work or promising ideas—what Mr. Fleishman would regard as "expressive." Many of these projects did improve society, or more precisely Jewish society, by enriching Jewish learning, observance, or charity. But the grants were not, in themselves, intended to engineer some change in the world. They bolstered new or ongoing programs that were inspiring, enterprising, well-run, and effective—and most of the time, for Mr. Fried and Mrs. Bernstein, that was reason enough to give.

A few projects, it's true, were more deliberately strategic and long-term, or "instrumental" by Mr. Fleishman's reckoning. The Jewish Community High School of the Bay, Nextbook/*Tablet,* and the orphanage projects in Russia and Ukraine all put the foundation front and center in an effort to transform a part of the Jewish landscape for the better. Establishing a pluralistic Jewish high school where none had existed; creating a new kind of sophisticated, wide-ranging publication of Jewish news and commentary; filling a void of compassionate Jewish care for Jewish children—all these followed the textbook foundation playbook: discerning a problem or gap, identifying the assets needed to solve the problem, and then pursuing that solution with sizable investments and hands-on strategic direction over several years.

But that is a very labor-intensive form of philanthropy, requiring constant monitoring, evaluation, and course-correction as work progresses and circumstances change. The high school and *Tablet*, in particular, absorbed much of Mr. Fried's and Mrs. Bernstein's time over many years (and *Tablet* continues to do so, though at a reduced level). The orphanages drew both trustees regularly to Russia, though in that case, the bulk of the management burden was borne by Chabad and Or Avner, organizations that were closer to the front lines. Linda Sakacs and Yehuda Novick provided additional oversight on all these projects, but the demands on Mrs. Bernstein and Mr. Fried were nonetheless extensive.

But these large, labor-intensive initiatives amounted to only slightly more than one-third of the foundation's total grantmaking in its first 20 years. In the remaining cases, Mr. Fried and Mrs. Bernstein may have sometimes devoted considerable attention to the progress of the work they supported—as they did, for example, in shaping the look and feel of MATACH's school libraries—but for the most part, they were content to rely on the talent and imagination of their grantees, the very qualities that had drawn them to these recipients in the first place.

In selecting grantees and deciding on the amounts of money awarded to each, almost nothing was more important to Mrs. Bernstein and Mr. Fried than the quality of the person or people leading an initiative. Time after time, in describing what drew them to make this or that grant, their comments turned to the vision, dedication, energy, and most of all, the proven record of the person or people at the top. In the foundation's many grants to advance Modern Orthodoxy, for example, it was Mr. Fried's and Mrs. Bernstein's firsthand observations of the talent of a rabbi or educator that persuaded them to donate. They had seen the scholar Micah Goodman and the rabbis Saul Berman, Avi Weiss, and Chaim Brovender in action, respected their work, and were confident of their ability to accomplish good things. It was mainly for that reason, and not because of any deep organizational analysis of Beit Prat, or Edah, or Yeshivat Chovevei Torah, or Midreshet Lindenbaum, that those institutions received major support from Keren Keshet.

Similarly, in choosing to help expand the Abraham Joshua Heschel School on the Upper West Side of Manhattan, the trustees of course took note of the school's excellent reputation, but their confidence was anchored in their high regard for then-head of school Roanna Shorofsky. "It was an outstanding school," Mrs. Bernstein said years later, "and she was terrific." The same was true of their confidence in Ruti Lehavi and her team at the Keshet School and of Rabbi Jeremy Stavisky at Himmelfarb High School. In speaking of Himmelfarb, for example, Mr. Fried zeroed in on "a dynamic principal who has provided the school with the Zionist spirit, with fine education, and with a spirit of service." He pointed to a telling detail: "In the period after Shavuot, when weddings are common, Rabbi Dr. Stavisky is booked months in advance to perform weddings for graduates of the school. Not their local rabbi, not their Rosh Yeshiva, not their Army rabbi, but this fine educator who had made such a great impression on them. It was Keren Keshet's privilege to support his work at the Himmelfarb High School."

All these grants plainly advanced the religious or educational missions of their respective institutions. But they were not what Mr. Fleishman would have called "instrumental," in that they were not made primarily to advance a strategy, solve a systemic problem, or reform some aspect of Jewish life. They were made to enable gifted Jewish educators and spiritual leaders to continue their work, reach more people, and draw additional support to their programs. The recipients of these grants also had the advantage of being well known to Mrs. Bernstein and Mr. Fried—personally in some cases, and by reputation in others. They were not chosen by a committee based on performance metrics or impact analytics.

And that is a direct result of how Mr. Fried and Mrs. Bernstein preferred to operate. If Keren Keshet had instead surveyed the entire field of Jewish education or Modern Orthodoxy or any other branch of Jewish communal life, searching for unknown talent and analyzing undetected gaps and trends, they might have made an additional grant or two. But that would have come at the expense of untold time and effort by a much larger staff or a battalion of consultants. That was simply not the trustees' idea of value. Nor was it their idea of how to conduct a joyful, helpful, and rewarding philanthropy. They preferred to govern their decision-making as much from the heart as from the brain.

"This was an expression of our own sense of what we wanted to do," Mr. Fried explained. "With Avi CHAI and with Tikvah, there were all these people, all these programs and policies. With Keren Keshet, there was nothing else. There was no one else. It has been a great pleasure, and it remains fun to this day."

Nonetheless, Keren Keshet's grantmaking was not all inspiration, fun, and exuberance. Its trustees also brought their own expertise and particular life experiences to the task, and part of the "great pleasure" they derived from it has been the result of drawing on their distinctive talents to make wise, creative, and disciplined use of the money available to them. Mr. Fried, a deft manager of philanthropies over nearly three decades, and before that a seasoned analyst, manager, and deal-maker in finance, had a keen eye for efficient and well-run organizations and the prudent use of funds. From long experience, he also knew how to create important buildings and build effective institutions.

Mrs. Bernstein had held senior leadership positions in Jewish communal organizations both nationally and in the San Francisco Bay Area, where she had lived and worked for many years. She moved at ease among major Jewish donors and felt at home in discussions of communal needs. She then had the opportunity, at Mr. Fried's side, to enroll in what amounted to a master class in the techniques of philanthropy, learning how to distinguish a credible project from one that promises too little or too much; how to scrutinize a budget and ferret out wishful thinking or simple excess; when to rely on expert opinion and when t0 trust one's native judgment and common sense; when to try to influence a grantee's choices and, more often, when to trust them to manage on their own.

"Everything was a 'we' project," Mrs. Bernstein said, describing her decades of friendship and partnership with Mr. Fried. "Everything was *we*. We made every decision together. We knew each other's interests, we relied on each other's judgment. We had enormous respect for each other." And from that merging of minds came the unusual combination of methodical and inspirational philanthropy that characterized Keren Keshet.

"Arthur made a philanthropist out of me," she concluded, with Mr.

Fried as usual by her side. "I had a lot to learn, but I had a great mentor. If either of us had been a different kind of person, it might have been awful. But we weren't, and the result was something great."

———

Beyond questions of philanthropic technique or style or forms of governance, Keren Keshet had one essential quality that, more than anything else, determined the kind of foundation it would be: It is a *Jewish* philanthropy, dedicated to Judaism, the Jewish people, and the Jewish state. That fact necessarily makes it, in Professor Fleishman's terms, an "expressive" institution, not "instrumental," because a commitment to Judaism arises from identity, belief, belonging, perseverance, and solidarity—adherence to a universal peoplehood that is neither a problem to be solved nor a campaign to be waged. It is, instead, an inherited treasure, "larger than oneself," to be cultivated, preserved, protected, strengthened, cherished, and celebrated.

The sometimes-improvisational nature of Keren Keshet's grantmaking—the lack of strategic restraints, the "warm hands" with which it gives, the "fun" the trustees experience in the giving—derives in part from a belief that supporting outstanding Jewish causes, leaders, ideas, and good works doesn't require field-mapping, Theories of Change, logic models, or any of the other complexities popular with philanthropic advisory firms. Rather, they consider a discerning and generous response to such opportunities, wherever they may happen to arise, an excellent form of Jewish philanthropy by itself, one that is also inspiring and rewarding. In their travels and their ongoing survey of the communal landscape, Mr. Fried and Mrs. Bernstein have constantly been alert to projects and programs, leaders and ideas, that could make Jewish lives better, richer, and more Jewish. And they have seized those opportunities wherever they could.

In his bare-bones formulation of Keren Keshet's philanthropy—
"do good; don't do bad; and Jewish"—Mr. Fried homed in on the
central, guiding principle of his and Mrs. Bernstein's work: the "single white light," from Abraham to today, that illuminates Jewish
schools and synagogues, books and concerts, artists and writers, students and sages, direct human charity and great institutional achievement. Support them—any of them, or many, or all of them—and you
help brighten the light for another generation.

Refracted through the miasma of contemporary society, through
the haze of secularism and multiculturalism, of technology and ideol-
ogy, the bright bands of color could, if untended, dissolve into a blur.
That they have not—that the many hues have remained vivid but
united in what Mr. Fried described, in Keren Keshet's incorporating
document, as "one common bond of purity and peace"—is the fruit
of three millennia of giving, tending, and nurturing. Keren Keshet
has taken its place, joyfully, warmly, but also diligently and circum-
spectly, in that long tradition of cultivation, and in the center of the
one warm light into which all the colors converge.

ACKNOWLEDGMENTS

Keren Keshet has been a nearly quarter-century-long labor of love by two people who relished the opportunity to support great Jewish causes and who willingly exerted the mental and emotional effort it took to provide that support wisely. Over the years, Arthur Fried, z"l, and Mem Bernstein mastered the art of personal, spontaneous, and diligent philanthropy with the aid of only a tiny staff, seeding hundreds of millions of dollars' worth of achievements in Jewish education, culture, religion, and other good works. When they asked me to undertake this history, I didn't hesitate to say yes. It is a joyful story, and a joy to tell.

That joy is mostly thanks to the many hours of warm, witty conversation that Mem and Arthur spent with me as I tried to understand how they went about finding opportunities, making decisions, and evaluating all they had done. But those conversations would not have been possible without months of prior research—primarily the volumes of archival records and data, and even more hours of candid reflections and explanation, that the foundation's three key staff members shared with me. Only because of the generosity and thoughtfulness of Linda Sakacs, Yehuda Novick, and Evan David Feinsilver was I able to assemble an accurate timeline of events and an accounting of grants and other outlays on which Mem and Arthur could then elaborate.

Keren Keshet's longest and most complicated project—which began life as Nextbook and today is called Tablet—was a fascinating challenge of storytelling unto itself. I could not have traced its evolution without the patient help of its founding director, Julie Sandorf; her successor, Morton Landowne; and Tablet's editor, Alana Newhouse. All three offered extensive reminiscences of their years of work on the project and frank assessments of all that it has accomplished. The first years of the Nextbook story were the subject of an earlier paper that I wrote for Julie, parts of which I have recapitulated here. Her colleagues on the project, especially book editor Jonathan Rosen and webmaster Blake Eskin, were bountiful sources of information and perspective in the months when I was compiling that original report.

Just as this book was completed, in April 2022, Arthur Fried passed away, leaving a giant hole in Jewish philanthropy and in the lives of many people—family, friends, employees, grantees, and admirers like me. My only disappointment in writing this volume is that he was never able to see the final draft. I hope he would have approved.

—Tony Proscio

NOTES

1. Rob Gloster, "The 2018 Portrait of Bay Area Jewish Life and Communities Shows Us Just Who We Are," The Jewish News of Northern California, Feb. 13, 2018, at https://www.jweekly.com/2018/02/13/first-ever-survey-entire-bay-area-paints-portrait-jewish-life/.
2. Joe Eskenazi, "Benefactor Purchases $20 Million S.F. Campus for JCHS," The Jewish News of Northern California, August 24, 2001, at https://www.jweekly.com/2001/08/24/benefactor-purchases-20-million-s-f-campus-for-jchs/.
3. BlueStarPR, "Year End Report," unpublished report to Keren Keshet—The Rainbow Foundation, Nov. 20, 2006, passim.
4. The three quotations in this paragraph are from BlueStarPR, op. cit., pp. 2, 6–7, and 6, respectively.
5. Eskenazi, op. cit.
6. Barbara Neufeld, with Rahel Wasserfal, "Jewish Community High School of the Bay: Making Strides Toward Jewish Continuity Through Day School Education," a report to Keren Keshet—The Rainbow Foundation, Education Matters, Sept. 2008, p. 55.
7. Ibid., p. 28.
8. Ibid., p. 17.
9. Ibid., p. 13.
10. Ibid., p. 14.
11. Ibid., p. 22.
12. Ibid., p. 23.
13. Ibid., p. 48.
14. Steven M. Cohen, "The Students and Alumni of the Jewish Community High School of the Bay: Findings, Lessons, and Implications of a Decade of Social Research," a report to Keren Keshet—The Rainbow Foundation, May 2019, p. 4.

15. Ibid., p. 7.
16. Ibid., p. 13.
17. Ibid. pp. 15–16.
18. Ibid., p. 34.
19. Ibid., p. 37.
20. Ibid. p. 73.
21. Ibid., p. 57.
22. Ibid., p. 6.
23. Ibid., p. 71.
24. Neufeld and Wasserfal, op. cit., p. 53.
25. Ibid., p. 52.
26. Ibid., p. 53.
27. Beginning here, this chapter borrows extensively from the author's work in two earlier reports: "Opening Pages: The origins of Nextbook and the start of a Jewish literary adventure," submitted to Keren Keshet—The Rainbow Foundation in June 2004, and "Nextbook's Second Chapter: Reflections on the 2004-05 Program Year," submitted February 2006.
28. Christopher Frizzelle, "Nextbook Disappears: The Only Organization Specifically Promoting Jewish Literature in Seattle," The Stranger, July 10, 2008, at https://www .thestranger.com/seattle/nextbook-disappears/Content?oid=615418.
29. Talila Nesher, "How to Say 'God' in the Classroom: Teaching for Religious Tolerance in Israel," Haaretz, March 31, 2013, accessed on 17 July 2015 at http://www.haaretz. com/news/israel/how-to-say-god-in-the-classroom-teaching-for-religious-tolerance -in-israel.premium-1.512803.
30. Rivkah Ginat, "Changing Israeli Society One School at a Time," The Jerusalem Post, March 20, 2014, at https://www.jpost.com/magazine/features/highlighting-rather -than-hiding-345971.
31. Jeremy Stavisky, "Challenges Facing Modern Orthodox Education in Israel," The Edah Journal, vol 4, no. 1, May 2004, at http://www.edah.org/backend/JournalArticle/4_1 _Stavisky.pdf.
32. Jeremy Stavisky, "Educating for Character and Leadership in an Israeli Religious High School," HaYidion: The Prizmah Journal, Prizmah Center for Jewish Day Schools, Summer 2010, pp. 58–59.
33. Shoshana London Sappir, "Profile: Tsila Hayun," Hadassah Magazine, January 2006, at https://www.hadassahmagazine.org/2006/01/11/profile-tsila-hayun/.
34. Ibid.
35. Zamir Choral Foundation, "HaZamir Chapters," at https://www.hazamir.org/about.
36. Ezra Kopelowitz, "Connecting to the Jewish People Through Singing: Survey of HaZamir: The International Jewish Teen Choir, Alumni and Current Singers," Research Success Technologies, April 2018, p. 2.
37. Peter Berkowitz, "Israel Program on Constitutional Government," web page at Prof. Berkowitz's website: http://www.peterberkowitz.com/ipcg.htm.
38. "The Chaim Weizmann Institute for the Study of Zionism and Israel," web page on the website for the Faculty of Humanities, Tel Aviv University: http://humanities1.tau. ac.il/zionism_eng/.
39. Metzila Center for Zionist, Jewish, Liberal, and Humanist Thought website, "About Metzila," at http://www.metzilah.org.il/847.
40. Pnima Israel website: https://www.pnimaisrael.com/english.

41. Beit Prat Israeli Midrasha website, the Mabua Program page, at https://beitprat.org /en-mabua-program/.

42. Jewish Virtual Library, "Ufa," from Encyclopedia Judaica, 2008, at https://www.jewish virtuallibrary.org/ufa.

43. Rena Udkoff, "From Heartbreak to Hope: Chabad Takes Children Off the Streets," Lubavitch International, Dec. 28, 2016, at https://www.lubavitch.com/from-heartbreak -to-hope/.

44. "New Wing for Jewish Children's Home in Moscow," Hamodia, April 9, 2019, at https://hamodia.com/2019/04/09/new-wing-jewish-childrens-home-moscow/.

45. Morton Landowne, "Entering Lincoln Square's Second Temple Period," The New York Jewish Week, Jan. 15, 2013, at https://jewishweek.timesofisrael.com/entering-lincoln -squares-second-temple-period/.

46. Joy Resmovits, "Iconic Synagogue on the Upper West Side Faces Tough Uphill Financial Battle," Forward, Oct. 15, 2010, at https://forward.com/news/132201/iconic -synagogue-on-the-upper-west-side-faces-toug/.

47. Landowne, op. cit.

48. CetraRuddy, "Lincoln Square Synagogue: Project Details," at http://cetraruddy.com /project/lincoln-square-synagogue.

49. Gary Rosenblatt, "If You Build It, Will They Come?" The New York Jewish Week, Jan. 2, 2013, at https://jewishweek.timesofisrael.com/if-you-build-it-will-they-come/.

50. David W. Dunlap, "With Eye on Tradition, a New Synagogue Opens," The New York Times, Jan. 28, 2013, p. A18.

51. "BimBam to Close This Spring After 11 Amazing Years as a Jewish Digital Storytelling Pioneer," BimBam press release, March 2019, at https://www.bimbam.com/bimbam-bids -farewell/.

52. "Bobbie's Place," The Chesed Fund website, at https://thechesedfund.com/bobbiesplace /fundraiser?aff=MATZAVARTICLE.

53. Joel L. Fleishman, The Foundation: A Great American Secret, PublicAffairs, 2007, pp. 47–48.

INDEX